PRAYING
the CATECHISM

PRAYING
the CATECHISM

Donald W. Johnson
and Susan C. Johnson

REVISED AND EXPANDED EDITION

 AUGSBURG FORTRESS

PRAYING THE CATECHISM
Revised and Expanded Edition

Cover and interior design: Tory Herman
Cover image: Green Branch. Seamless Pattern iStock/ajuga
Interior art: Gertrud Mueller Nelson
Typesetting: Eileen Engebretson

Manufactured in the USA.

ISBN 978-1-5064-8012-1

30 29 28 27 26 25 24 23 22 21   1 2 3 4 5 6 7 8 9 10

CONTENTS

FOREWORD

My dad, Pastor Donald W. Johnson, wrote *Praying the Catechism* twenty-five years ago. At his funeral two years ago, the preacher invited us all to reread this book and to let my father continue to teach us. As I began to read again the words of Martin Luther and my father, the idea for this new edition entered my head.

I have long been concerned about the need for both a spiritual renewal in our churches and a focus on discipleship practices: prayer, scripture reading, diaconal service to those who are in need or are marginalized, stewardship of the earth and of our personal finances, the ability to comfortably share our faith. With increasingly busy lives we have lost much of the teaching function of the church. How then to help people learn how to pray and to walk more closely with God?

Martin Luther's Small Catechism was written to help people gather in their homes to learn about their faith and to deepen their relationship with God. The catechism still works as a solid framework for that purpose. Similarly, I was impressed with how well my father's words still speak to us even twenty-five years later.

In this edition of *Praying the Catechism*, I have updated some examples and language. Things have changed, both in our churches and in our societies, in the last quarter century! I have also added a prayer at the end of each day's devotion. As I have spoken to people across the church and around the world, I have found that there is great hesitancy about praying. People have told me that they don't know whether they are praying correctly. I get it; I used to worry about grammar police waiting to pounce on me. But over the years I have learned that there is no right way to pray—what a relief! My prayers are meant to be examples to help you begin praying each day. Talk to God honestly from your heart. That's all you need to do!

I write this during the time of the COVID-19 pandemic. For most of us, daily life has changed dramatically. Lockdowns, wearing masks, self-isolating, social distancing, widespread unemployment, food insecurity and hunger, working from home, helping children with remote learning—it feels like a different world. Now more than ever, we need the comfort and strength of our faith. We need our relationship with God. I hope this book will help you to explore your faith, to deepen your prayer life, and to invigorate your relationship with God. Working on this new edition has strengthened my faith.

I am praying for you, and for all who seek to follow the Holy One, in Jesus' name. Amen.

+ Susan C. Johnson
National Bishop, Evangelical Lutheran Church in Canada
February 2021

INTRODUCTION TO
THE ORIGINAL EDITION

Martin Luther, the sixteenth-century reformer, faced the challenge of education for lay people. To meet this challenge, he wrote a catechism for use in family prayer and in private meditation. For many years his work has been used in this manner and has had a profound influence on the life of the church.

In more recent years Luther's Small Catechism, with its discussion of the Ten Commandments, the Apostles' Creed, the Lord's Prayer, the Sacrament of Holy Baptism, Confession, and the Sacrament of the Altar, has been used for teaching. Taking the catechism from the prayer room to the classroom has changed it, however, for it has become a focus of indoctrination rather than a focus of devotion.

This devotional book is an attempt to restore the Small Catechism to the prayer room. It invites you to experience the catechism through a journey of prayer and meditation. Along with the catechism, passages from scripture and from the liturgies of baptism and the eucharist are used as a starting point for some meditations.

This book was written to be a part of the Adult Catechumenate Program of the Evangelical Lutheran Church in Canada, for adults preparing for baptism. It is divided into two sections that may be used approximately forty days before and fifty days after baptism. If baptism is to occur at the Easter Vigil, the two sections are especially appropriate for the seasons of Lent and Easter, respectively. It is hoped that people preparing to affirm their faith, whether old or young, might find this book helpful.

It is also hoped that this book will be used by individuals and families as part of devotional life. In this case, the book may be used in its ninety-day entirety, or the devotions may be undertaken through the six sections of the catechism: the Ten Commandments, the Apostles' Creed, the Lord's Prayer, Baptism, Confession, and the Sacrament of the Altar.

This book has been written for the community of Gloria Dei Lutheran Church, North Vancouver, British Columbia. I wish to thank the members of this parish who have provided generous feedback as this book was being prepared. Three people deserve special thanks: Lois Johnson, Erika Kingston, and Lois Grierson, for their help in editing and typing.

Donald W. Johnson
North Vancouver, BC
Canada

SUGGESTIONS
FOR DAILY USE

You are invited to enter a journey of daily prayer and meditation. This is an important discipline in the Christian life. It is not always easy. There are six meditations for each week, from Monday to Saturday. Each Sunday you are encouraged to join the members of your parish for prayer in worship.

Begin each day by recognizing that you are in the presence of God. Ask God to help and guide you in your daily time of prayer. Always seek to discover God's graciousness in the day.

Follow this by reading the quotation at the beginning of each meditation and taking a moment for reflection. What do these words say to you at this time in your life?

When you are ready, go on to the "Pause and Reflect" section of the meditation. You may again ponder how this touches your life. In what way is the God of grace speaking to you today?

If you are reading this prayer book within the context of a family or household, you may wish to use this time for some group discussion.

Close each period of meditation with prayer. Use the prayer suggestions as you wish, but you will soon discover that there is much more for you to pray about.

What length of time should you take for each period of prayer? Find out what works best for you, and do not rush. Take time to enjoy being in the presence of God.

You may be a part of a community of people preparing for baptism or for the service of Affirmation of Baptism. Pray for them each day, and participate in the fellowship of prayer with them.

This book comes with space for you to write or cartoon your responses. This will help you to look back over the week and recall what has been happening within you. If you are using this book with others, these are some of the things that you might be able to share with that group.

To pray is to learn to love God and enjoy the presence of God. To pray is to learn to watch for the things that are happening within you and around you each day, and to come to see them as part of the gifts of God. To pray is to anticipate God's blessing.

NO OTHER GODS ✦ ✦ ✦
The Ten Commandments

DAY I, MONDAY

I am the LORD your God, who brought you out of the land of Egypt, out of the house of slavery.

Exodus 20:2

PAUSE AND REFLECT

God speaks to Moses: *Remember, first, that I am the God who has rescued you.* In light of this great rescue, the commandments are then given. This same mysterious God spoke to Moses earlier in the burning bush, saying, *I have heard the people's cries. I know their suffering and I will rescue them.* At the heart of the ten commandments and of this covenant is the God of compassion who delivers people.

We all have some type of image of God. For some, the ten commandments evoke an image of judgment, strict discipline, or punishment for stepping over the line. The ten commandments, however, begin with a word about the God who rescues. First God rescues us, then speaks the ten commandments.

In what ways has God rescued you? What gifts of deliverance has God given you? You may remember times in your life when you experienced God's hand of deliverance.

Where are you still struggling to be freed? From racism? From transphobia or homophobia? From gender oppression? From workaholism? From addiction?

PRAY

- Spend some time thanking God for deliverance you have experienced.
- Pray for others who seek the deliverance of God in their lives: the sick, the poor, the addicted, and the dying.
- If you are enslaved in some way, ask God to rescue you.

God of freedom, you continue to bring us out of oppression. We pray that those who would still enslave us would let us go, so that they too will be free. Enable us to experience your liberating grace in our daily lives. In the name of Jesus we pray. Amen.

DAY 2, TUESDAY

The LORD said, ". . . I have come down to deliver [the people] from the Egyptians, and to bring them up out of that land to a good and broad land, a land flowing with milk and honey."

Exodus 3:7, 8

PAUSE AND REFLECT

The God of the ten commandments is one who gives gifts. We often think of commandments or rules as burdens that restrict us. The ten commandments, however, come from a God who gives gifts.

These commandments are gift.

Israel came to understand that the whole of life was gift. To believe in this God was to see life as gift. The world, daily bread, my property, myself, and my whole life is gift. All of creation takes on a different meaning when acknowledged as gift. My mother and father, my spouse, my children, siblings, neighbours, and possessions take on a different character when seen as gift. Even my enemies take on a new character when I dare to pronounce them as gift.

Think of all of your own past as gift. Consider the people and the things that surround your present life as gift. Consider this: The God who gives gifts will be present in the future, so you really have nothing to fear.

Are we who are part of God's covenant with the Israelites also on a pilgrimage to a land flowing with milk and honey? Will we be embraced by these gifts throughout our lives?

What does it mean that all people do not receive the same gifts? When it comes to the basics needed for life, how does that call us to work for redistribution and justice?

It's sometimes hard to see life as gift in times of adversity—illness, death, pandemic, job loss, the end of a relationship, and so on. How can we look for gifts from God in difficult times?

PRAY

+ Give thanks for people, possessions, and the world of nature that God has given to us as gift.
+ Invite God to help you to see yourself as gift and to see your purpose for being placed on the earth.
+ Thank God for the ten commandments.

Liberating God, you continue to give us life and to gift us with good things. Help us to see and to embrace your gifts and your goodness in our daily lives, even in hard times. Open us to receive and appreciate the gift of the ten commandments. In your life-giving name we pray. Amen.

DAY 3, WEDNESDAY

"If you love me, you will keep my commandments."
John 14:15

PAUSE AND REFLECT

What holds families together? Is it rules and regulations? What holds a couple together? Is it obedience to a contract each signed when they married? What holds a nation together? Is it the strong arm of the law?

Jesus knows that caring or loving is the most powerful factor in holding people in relationships. This is also true for our relationship with God. It is not fear of punishment that holds us to the ten commandments. The commandments are given to people who have been rescued by the God whose basic character is one of love for the whole of creation, including each person in that creation.

How can the people of God show their love for God and love for neighbour? That is the basic question of the commandments. Love for God is expressed directly to God in words and through your neighbour and the rest of the creation. If love is removed from the commandments, you have only empty rules.

Do you love God? Perhaps the first question to ask is, Does God love you?

PRAY

+ Be still before God. Ask God to show you the depth of the love God has for you.
+ Pray for those preparing to be baptized and for those who will affirm their baptism.
+ Pray for those who do not yet know God's love. Pray that God in mercy will pour out the Spirit of love to all.

Generous God, your love for us—each one of us—is wide and deep, passionate and tender, and ever faithful. We thank you for this gift. Help us to love you with our whole hearts, and to share your love with our neighbours. In your loving name we pray. Amen.

DAY 4, THURSDAY

The First Commandment

You shall have no other gods.

WHAT IS THIS? *or* WHAT DOES THIS MEAN?

We are to fear, love, and trust God above all things.
(SC)

PAUSE AND REFLECT

Paul Tillich, a theologian, taught that people attach themselves to something that gives their lives purpose and meaning. What gives your life purpose? Is it family, work, possessions, political theories, economic theories? Who or what is number one in your life? Your looks or health or fitness; having a good time at all costs; buying new things; future security; country; church; work; youth; travel; vacations; your children; your boat; or your car? All of these things invite us to have them at the centre of our lives.

Luther wrote that we should fear and love God above all things. To fear is to stand before the mystery and wonder of God. To fear is to stand under the stars at night and consider the vastness of creation. To fear is to stand by the power of ocean waves and understand the power of water and of the God who stands over and above and for creation. To fear is to stand in wonder over the population of the world, with its billions, and recognize that God knows and cares for each person in the same way that God cares for you.

To fear is to recognize that there is a difference between the Creator and yourself and that you will not comprehend the full mystery of God.

We should fear and love God above all things. We should love God when we see this mysterious God revealed in the history of Israel and in the person of Jesus Christ. We respond to God with love as we grow in understanding of God's deep affection for us and for the world. This God is the only one. All others are exposed to be false in the presence of this God.

Other gods (including things we list as number one in our lives) have the power to tempt, capture, and control us. If they are more important to us than God, then they are false gods. In baptism we renounce these false gods:

> Do you renounce the devil and all the forces that defy God?
> **I renounce them.**
>
> Do you renounce the powers of this world that rebel against God?
> **I renounce them.**
>
> Do you renounce the ways of sin that draw you from God?
> **I renounce them.**[1]

This is a lifelong journey.

PRAY

+ Make a list of who or what is most important in your life at this time. Are there changes you would like to make to this list?

+ Pray for false gods to have less power in your life.

+ Pray for people struggling with addiction.

God, we want to love you with our whole hearts. We confess that sometimes other things consume our time, our energy, and our finances. Help us to keep our lives in balance and to fear, love, and trust you above all other things. In your holy name we pray. Amen.

DAY 5, FRIDAY

The Second Commandment

*You shall not make wrongful use
of the name of the Lord your God.*

WHAT IS THIS? *or* WHAT DOES THIS MEAN?

*We are to fear and love God,
so that we do not curse, swear, practice magic,
lie, or deceive using God's name,
but instead use that very name
in every time of need
to call on, pray to, praise, and give thanks to God.*
(SC)

PAUSE AND REFLECT

Your surname speaks of your family history, and your given name gives you a personal identity in that history. When people love you, they use your name in endearing ways. They speak it in affection. Some may give you a nickname. Others use your name to dishonour or disrespect you.

When you love a person, you treasure their name. How does your use of the names God, Lord, Jesus, Saviour, and Christ reflect your love of God?

How do you use God's name? Do you use it to curse others, to hide the truth, to pretend while making promises, to deceive others about your real intent or your real self? What does it mean that the use of OMG ("Oh my God") has become so common that we use it without thinking?

Paul said, "Bless those who persecute you; bless and do not curse them" (Romans 12:14). Use God's name to bless, to praise, and to build up. Use God's name to pray, to praise, and to offer thanksgiving.

This commandment, like all others, is given to the community of faith. At times we grow careless—careless about words, about people, about nature, about our

20

possessions, and about truth. But to be a follower of Christ is to be careful about people, about creation, and even about names.

All are invited to call on God by using the divine name. You might notice that God's name is used in many places as a cry for help. Lord, enable us to hear those cries.

PRAY

+ Spend some time recalling or looking for names for God that are used in the scriptures.
+ Pray for the church around the world as it honours the name of God in prayers of praise and thanksgiving.
+ Spend some time reflecting on how and when you refer to God. Is there anything you might want to change about this?

God, you love us so much that you tenderly call us by name. Help us to use your name in ways that show you love and honour. In your holy name we pray. Amen.

DAY 6, SATURDAY

The Third Commandment

Remember the sabbath day, and keep it holy.

WHAT IS THIS? *or* WHAT DOES THIS MEAN?

We are to fear and love God,
so that we do not despise preaching or God's word,
but instead keep that word holy
and gladly hear and learn it. (SC)

PAUSE AND REFLECT

Today's culture encourages us to fill each moment with sound, excitement, and activities. Work is ever-present, and labour-saving devices simply grant us more "freedom" to get out and work to pay for them. Part-time jobs without benefits and the gig economy mean many people work seven days a week. Work, stress, and family responsibilities lead us to ever-increasing busyness with no time to stop and listen or pray. Holidays too are often overly busy, as we expend so much energy living up to our own or other people's expectations or standards that we end up exhausted. There is no time for buildings, land, creation, and people to rest or to be restored, and certainly little time for the quiet and relaxation that might allow us to listen for God's voice.

In contrast to all of this, the third commandment invites rest, prayer, renewal, and restoration. For the people of Israel, who had been enslaved in Egypt, the new covenant represented by the ten commandments was one of rest and trust—trust that the gifts of God would be given in the rhythm of work and rest and prayer.

During Martin Luther's day there were many holy days and days of rest. For Luther, the third commandment encouraged the sharing of God's word and the gathering of the community on these days.

Perhaps in our day we need to again emphasize a sabbath as a day of rest and the sharing of God's word and sacraments in community. In this commandment God calls us to a rhythm of work and leisure, of praise and prayer, of time alone and time in community—a rhythm that calls for trust in God to provide for all our needs.

Remember the sabbath, remember rest, remember prayer, remember God's word, remember the sacraments, and remember the God who speaks in times of quiet.

PRAY

+ Confess to the Lord any busyness that leaves no time for God, for family, for friends, for neighbours, and for care of the earth.
+ Pray for people under stress from overwork.
+ Pray for times of rest and times of quiet.

God, we confess that sometimes we are so busy that we squeeze you in after everything else is done. Make us aware of your presence with us throughout the day and night. Help us to take time for rest and renewal, time for prayer, and time to join with others in listening to your word and in being fed by your sacraments. In your life-giving and restoring name we pray. Amen.

DAY 7, SUNDAY

This is the day set aside to join the gathered community for prayer and worship. Spend time praying for the people, the pastors, and all who offer their gifts in worship. Pray that all hearts will be open to the word of God. If possible, read in advance the scripture texts for today's worship. Look for Revised Common Lectionary texts in *Evangelical Lutheran Worship* (pages 18–63), or ask your pastor for a list of upcoming scripture readings.

PRAY

Holy God, we pray for those who will gather for worship today. We pray for those who will lead in worship and share God's word. We pray that this time of worship will be a blessing for those who gather. We also pray for those who are not able to join in worship—those who are working, those who are ill. Help them to find ways to hear your saving word today. In Jesus' name we pray. Amen.

DAY 8, MONDAY

The Fourth Commandment

Honor your father and your mother.

WHAT IS THIS? *or* WHAT DOES THIS MEAN?

We are to fear and love God,
so that we neither despise nor anger
our parents and others in authority,
but instead honor, serve, obey,
love, and respect them. (SC)

PAUSE AND REFLECT

Honour your father and mother. In some cases there is so much abuse, so much neglect, so much isolation, and so little help within a family. If you have grown up with this, God's healing comes in the midst of facing the truth. You will not honour anyone by keeping things hidden.

If you have grown up in a family where parents or caregivers have been loving, caring, and supportive, it is easier to honour them. Have you thanked God and others for this gift?

Martin Luther extends this fourth commandment to more than family relationships—to all authorities in courts, governments, schools, and police. These authorities are given to all by God for the task of governance. But again, as in families, we learn early on that authorities do not always follow the will of God by seeking the common good. Do we honour if we rally around the flag to proclaim, "My country, right or wrong"? Do we honour with unquestioning political support for elected and appointed officials? Do we honour by claiming the rights of the privileged when this endangers the good—or even the survival—of many?

This commandment is an invitation to you. You are called to be an agent of reconciliation in all areas of your life. You are called to enter into a covenant of truth with others.

These are good, gentle, and hard ways in which you might follow Christ:

+ "Do not let the sun go down on your anger" (Ephesians 4:26).

+ "If another member of the church sins against you, go and point out the fault" (Matthew 18:15).

+ "Forgive each other; just as the Lord has forgiven you" (Colossians 3:13).

+ "Speaking the truth in love, we must grow up in every way into . . . Christ" (Ephesians 4:15).

+ "Do not repay anyone evil for evil" (Romans 12:17).

PRAY

+ Pray for families and for those in distress.

+ Pray for survivors of abuse.

+ Pray for church leaders and for governmental authorities.

+ Thank God for help and support from people.

God, you call us into many relationships and ask us to honour those in places of authority. Teach us to show love and respect within our families. Help us to forgive others when they make mistakes. Guide us to support those who share the pain of abuse, and to hold perpetrators to accountability. Embolden us to speak truth to power when authority is misused. In your loving name we pray. Amen.

DAY 9, TUESDAY

The Fifth Commandment
You shall not murder.

WHAT IS THIS? *or* WHAT DOES THIS MEAN?

We are to fear and love God,
so that we neither endanger nor harm
the lives of our neighbors,
but instead help and support them
in all of life's needs. (SC)

PAUSE AND REFLECT

Toxic waste is a way of killing.
Hunger is a way of killing.
Poverty is a way of killing.
War is a way of killing.
Racial discrimination is a way of killing.
Putting resources into excessive armaments, and not into health, is a way of killing.

O Lord, we have devised so many ways of killing.

Exploiting the environment is a way of killing.
Abuse (sexual, physical, and emotional) is a way of killing.
Addictive substances are a way of killing.
Drinking and driving can be a way of killing.
Selling expired medicine to the poor can be a way of killing.
Withholding health care is a way of killing.
Unemployment is a way of killing.
Selling powdered formula to people without clean water can be a way of killing.

But also, telling someone they are ugly is a way of killing.
Making fun of people is a way of killing.
Racial slurs are a way of killing.

O Lord, we have devised so many ways of killing. Help us to understand that as citizens of the global village we have responsibility for preserving and supporting life.

Guide us to find creative ways to support the lives of people on this planet. Help us to follow this call of Jesus each day:

> Come, you that are blessed by my Father, inherit the kingdom prepared for you from the foundation of the world; for I was hungry and you gave me food, I was thirsty and you gave me something to drink, I was a stranger and you welcomed me, I was naked and you gave me clothing, I was sick and you took care of me, I was in prison and you visited me. (Matthew 25:34-36)

What can you do to support the lives of those around you?

PRAY

+ Pray for the unemployed.

+ Pray for those who work for justice and peace.

+ Pray for those who work in health care, food banks, welfare offices.

+ Pray for those who protect the environment.

+ Pray for those who grow food for the hungry.

God of life, you call us to love our neighbour, and you put before us choices of life and death, blessings and curses. Help us to choose life and love in our relationships with all people and all creation. Guard and guide our words and our deeds so that we do not harm people near or far. We pray in your loving and life-giving name. Amen.

DAY 10, WEDNESDAY

The Sixth Commandment

You shall not commit adultery.

WHAT IS THIS? *or* WHAT DOES THIS MEAN?

We are to fear and love God,
so that we lead pure and decent lives
in word and deed,
and each of us loves and honors his or her spouse.
(SC)

PAUSE AND REFLECT

Sexuality is a wonderful and powerful gift. It binds couples together in intimacy and love. It flows through us and in us into everything that we do. God created many of us for loving, intimate partnerships. God calls us into families.

Yet wonderful and powerful gifts, when given into the control of false gods, can result in much pain, hurt, and abuse. The powerful gift of sexuality is given to us, and we are called to choose: Shall we use the gift to build up and support? Or shall we use the gift to control, to exploit, and to bring division?

We are a people in deep trouble with sexuality. There is so much abuse of women and children. Some people struggle with their sexual orientation, gender identity, or gender expression. Some people struggle to accept those with differing sexual orientations, gender identities, or gender expressions. Some people ignore the vows of faithfulness that they or others have made. Some people make a living exploiting the sexuality of others.

Perhaps it is because we have too often given ourselves over to the gods of consumerism that we have come to see our sexuality as a commodity. There is a wonderful image in the Bible of the children of Israel being led from the land of Egypt, where they were abused, to a new land of promise. God longs to lead us to a land flowing with milk and honey, where our sexuality will add to our fullness of life, and not be the centre of such pain, abuse, and exploitation.

Two people stand before a Christian community at worship and make promises to one another to become spouses. The community promises to celebrate their love, to honour their marriage, and to help them when they have trouble.

This is the kind of help and support that we can give to others as we seek to follow the rescuing God out of the bondage of our sin and into the new land where our sexuality will again be celebrated as gift. God calls you on this journey.

PRAY

+ Pray for couples in trouble.
+ Pray for those who live alone.
+ Pray for God to strengthen you in your relationships.
+ Pray for people who are caught in a web of abuse.
+ Pray for your congregation, that it may be a place of healing and support for all people regardless of sexual orientation, gender identity, or gender expression.
+ Pray for those who are persecuted because of their sexual orientation or gender identity.

Loving God, you create us in your image: straight, lesbian, gay, bisexual, transgender, cisgender, agender, queer, questioning, two-spirit, intersex, and gender-fluid. You give us the gift of sexuality to treasure and use in a way that respects ourselves and others. You call us to care for and support other people in their relationships. Help us to be strong, loving, and wise in the ways we relate to one another. In your loving name we pray. Amen.

DAY 11, THURSDAY

The Seventh Commandment

You shall not steal.

WHAT IS THIS? *or* WHAT DOES THIS MEAN?

We are to fear and love God,
so that we neither take our neighbors' money
or property
nor acquire them by using shoddy merchandise
or crooked deals,
but instead help them to improve and protect
their property and income. (SC)

PAUSE AND REFLECT

Inflation steals.

Excess profits steal.

Forcing people to be refugees steals.

Income-tax cheating steals.

Government mismanagement steals.

Unemployment steals.

Vandalism steals.

Unjust wages steal.

Polluting the environment steals.

Careless exploitation of land and resources steals.

Destroying property steals.

In the seventh commandment we are invited to resist the temptation to steal, and to protect our neighbours' property and living. As in all the other commandments, we are called to use care in dealing with our neighbours. We are to be careful—full of care—when it comes to our neighbours' house and property, for these are intimately connected to their lives.

There are many ways to help our neighbours care for property. For example, how many more elders would be able to remain in their own homes if increased efforts were made to help them look after their property?

Sometimes care of neighbour requires group action. Can you join groups that protect property and the environment, or support such groups in prayer?

Other gods rule our age, inviting us to be careless about property. Our throwaway society carries this mindset into every aspect of our lives, including care for the property of others. Imagine what it would have been like if the early settlers in North America had been concerned about protecting the property of those who already lived here. What would this land be like now?

We need a new spirit to blow into the dry bones of our disposable society, to call us again to new life. Pray for the Spirit to do this work in you and in your neighbours.

PRAY

+ Pray for those who work for justice and peace.
+ Pray for the nation, that all may come to see land and property as gift.
+ Pray for refugees who suffer loss and displacement.
+ Pray for your neighbour.
+ Give thanks for Indigenous peoples who have stewarded the land for thousands of years.

Merciful God, we confess that we are too often influenced by our society and put ourselves and our wants first, even at the expense of our neighbour. We confess our selfishness that allows us to enter into forms of stealing and to delude ourselves that what we are doing is right. Help us to care for the possessions of our neighbours, including all of creation. We pray in Jesus' name. Amen.

DAY 12, FRIDAY

The Eighth Commandment
You shall not bear false witness against your neighbor.

WHAT IS THIS? *or* WHAT DOES THIS MEAN?

We are to fear and love God,
so that we do not tell lies about our neighbors,
betray or slander them,
or destroy their reputations.
Instead we are to come to their defense,
speak well of them,
and interpret everything they do
in the best possible light. (SC)

PAUSE AND REFLECT

"Sticks and stones may break my bones, but words will never hurt me." As a child, did you shout this old adage at the kids next door when they called you names and made you angry? Unfortunately, it is not true: words do have the power to hurt and injure.

Gossip is one of the chief causes of strife in congregations and communities. People talk *about* other people, but do not talk *to* them about the hurt or concern. "Don't tell anyone, but . . ." "I know I shouldn't be telling you this . . ." "Have you heard about . . . ?" It is easy for us to heap vengeance on those who have done wrong to us by complaining to others and by speaking about our neighbour in the worst way. Often we are aware this will hurt our neighbour, and that is what we intend. Sometimes we are unaware. Lord, forgive us.

Christ calls us to a new life that includes a ministry of reconciliation. Instead of spreading gossip, lies, and misinformation, we are to speak highly of our neighbour and explain their actions in the kindest way. We make a new covenant in our families and in our communities: "If you have offended me, I will tell you. And if I have offended you, you must tell me."

Let us live the new life to which God is calling us.

PRAY

+ Pray for those who are injured by the telling of true and false tales.

+ Pray for your parish in its work of reconciliation.

+ Pray for those who work in news media, that they will use accurate and fair reporting.

+ Pray for our leaders, that they will work in ways of truth and justice.

+ Pray for those who use social media, that they do so in ways that respect others.

God of truth, we confess the times that we have indulged in gossip and the spreading of tales. We acknowledge the harm that we have done, and we humbly repent. Help us to use our voices to build up—and not tear down—relationships and community. Guide us to speak in ways of truth and justice. In your holy name we pray. Amen.

DAY 13, SATURDAY

The Ninth Commandment
You shall not covet your neighbor's house.

WHAT IS THIS? *or* WHAT DOES THIS MEAN?

We are to fear and love God,
so that we do not try to trick our neighbors
out of their inheritance or property
or try to get it for ourselves
by claiming to have a legal right to it and the like,
but instead be of help and service to them
in keeping what is theirs. (SC)

PAUSE AND REFLECT

Our world runs on consumerism. We are encouraged every day to covet, to fulfill every want.

The gods of consumerism are strong and very tempting with their insidious appeal to our egos that if we eat the right food, drink the right drink, drive the right car, live in the right home, and choose the right painkiller, we could achieve a new level of fulfillment.

But God promises to fulfill our every need, not our every want.

For most people, there is no difference between a want and a need. The result is that we think nothing of buying whatever we want. There is an ecological cost, however, to excessive consumerism. Producing everything involved in meeting our wants takes resources and energy, and adds to the pollution of the globe.

While pastors hear many types of confession today, they rarely hear someone confess to covetousness. In fact, it appears that we have made covetousness a virtue: "We are going to have to spend our way out of the recession." "Be a good citizen and buy, so that the economy will get going again." Thus sin is paraded as virtue. Lord, have mercy on us all.

Excessive consumerism touches everything. It has even touched Christianity. It has taught us to spend money on ourselves first, rather than treating money as a gift from God and using it to generously give back to God and help others. People are invited to come to Jesus or come to worship for what they can get out of it. And we dare not speak of the Christian way as taking up the cross, lest we drive religious shoppers elsewhere.

What would happen if we focused more on the needs of all people than on our wants?

PRAY

+ Pray that the Spirit will help you to understand the difference between need and want.
+ Pray for yourself and our society, that all may be delivered from the slavery of consumerism.
+ Pray for those who do not have their basic needs met.
+ Pray for a just distribution of wealth and for all kinds of work to be valued.
+ Pray that God would make our hearts generous, so that we give glory to God and help our neighbour.

Loving God, we confess the ways we give in to greed. We confess that we do not always know the difference between our needs and our wants. We confess that we look to our own desires, sometimes at the expense of others. Give us generous hearts to ensure that the basic needs of all people are met. Help us to live simpler and more sustainable lives. We pray in Jesus' name. Amen.

DAY 14, SUNDAY

This is Sunday. You can prepare yourself for worship by reading the scripture texts set aside for this day. Pray for your community and the other churches in your area that will also gather for worship.

PRAY

Holy God, we give thanks for the opportunity to come together and worship you this day. Open our hearts and minds to be aware of your presence and hear your word. Help us to be fully present and attentive to the words of the hymns, liturgy, readings, prayers, and sermon, and to hear what you are saying to us this day. Keep us from being distracted from you, especially with thoughts that would break your commandments. We pray in your life-giving name. Amen.

DAY 15, MONDAY

The Tenth Commandment

You shall not covet your neighbor's wife,
or male or female slave, or ox, or donkey,
or anything that belongs to your neighbor.

WHAT IS THIS? *or* WHAT DOES THIS MEAN?

We are to fear and love God,
so that we do not entice, force,
or steal away from our neighbors
their spouses, household workers, or livestock,
but instead urge them to stay
and fulfill their responsibilities to our neighbors. (SC)

PAUSE AND REFLECT

God must have known that this sin of covetousness would be insidious in our day, because it is mentioned twice in the commandments. If you live in the country, you understand about coveting land and cattle. If you live in the city, you know about coveting jobs and homes. We all know about coveting another's spouse. Here again, we struggle with what we need and what we want.

If you want to hire your neighbour's workers, is it not common practice to simply offer them more money? It is hard to imagine that you would encourage those workers to stay with their present employer.

We have convinced ourselves that we live in a tough, "dog-eat-dog" world, and that if we show care for another company, or another university, or another church, we will be suspect. Rather than seeing all people as God's children, we may even go so far as to think of them as commodities that can help us on the way to success. Rescue us, Lord, as you rescued the Israelites from slavery in Egypt.

Look for others in your parish who are concerned about these things. Talk about what needs to change for the good of all, and about your hopes and dreams for a new age.

PRAY

+ Pray for spouses, that their lives together may be supported by friends and neighbours.

+ Pray for a new way to look at people as beloved children of God to treasure, and not as competitors or as individuals to be used for personal gain.

+ Pray for those who are to be baptized, that they, and we, may be washed of sin. Pray that new life in God will arise in all the baptized.

Gracious God, you give us so many gifts, and yet we always seem to want more. Curb our voracious appetites. Help us to be satisfied with who we are and what we have. Guide us to lift up the well-being of others instead of seeing them as competitors or rivals. Lead us in living lives of thanksgiving. In Jesus' name we pray. Amen.

DAY 16, TUESDAY

You shall have no other gods.
You shall not make wrongful use of the name of the
Lord your God.
Remember the sabbath day, and keep it holy.
Honor your father and your mother.
You shall not murder.
You shall not commit adultery.
You shall not steal.
You shall not bear false witness against your neighbor.
You shall not covet your neighbor's house.
You shall not covet your neighbor's wife, or male
or female slave, or ox, or donkey, or anything that
belongs to your neighbor.

PAUSE AND REFLECT

The gods of our age are strong. They promise much, but bring only death. God calls you to walk a new life.

On Ash Wednesday the people of God in various communities gather for a service of confession. We gather in the hope that something new can arise out of the ashes of our lives. If possible, pray your way through the Ash Wednesday litany of confession (*Evangelical Lutheran Worship* [ELW], pages 252–253).

During the past several days you have been asked to reflect on your life and the ten commandments. Where have you "sinned in thought, word, and deed, by what [you] have done and by what [you] have left undone"?[2] Are you able to acknowledge the harm you may have caused? Are there apologies or reparations you need to make, or fences you need to mend?

PRAY

+ Pray for forgiveness for harm you have caused, and for the strength and guidance to live a new life.

+ Pray for the courage and strength to make amends to people you have hurt.

Forgiving God, we confess that we do not always say or do the things that follow both the words and the spirit of your commandments. Where we have done wrong, forgive us, renew us, and lead us in new ways that follow the example of Jesus. We pray this in a spirit of humility and repentance, and in the name of Jesus. Amen.

I BELIEVE ... ✦ ✦ ✦
The Apostles' Creed

DAY 17, WEDNESDAY

The Apostles' Creed

I believe in God, the Father almighty,
   creator of heaven and earth.

I believe in Jesus Christ, God's only Son, our Lord,
   who was conceived by the Holy Spirit,
   born of the virgin Mary,
   suffered under Pontius Pilate,
   was crucified, died, and was buried;
   he descended to the dead.
   On the third day he rose again;
   he ascended into heaven,
   he is seated at the right hand of the Father,
   and he will come to judge the living and the dead.

I believe in the Holy Spirit,
   the holy catholic Church,
   the communion of saints,
   the forgiveness of sins,
   the resurrection of the body,
   and the life everlasting. Amen. (SC)

PAUSE AND REFLECT

The Apostles' Creed proclaims the foundation of the life of every Christian. This is the creed included in all baptisms. While the ten commandments speak of other gods, the creed expresses the basic Christian understanding of God. As we baptize an adult, the person says, "This is what I believe." As we baptize a child, the parents and congregation say, "This is the God this child will come to love and follow." At baptism, water is poured in the name of the Father, and the Son, and the Holy Spirit.

Each time Christians gather for worship in the name of the Trinity, the Apostles' Creed or something similar is proclaimed. Through these words we are called to remember our baptism and the God in whose name we are baptized.

When you die, the paschal candle of baptism will be lit. The faithful will gather and remind one another of the faith by saying the Apostles' Creed as they commend you to God.

Through your reflection and prayers over the next few days, you will be invited to treasure this creed in which the believing church announces to the world, "We believe in this God."

PRAY

+ Pray for the church around the world as it confesses the faith.
+ Pray for people who are making final preparations for baptism or affirmation of baptism.
+ Give thanks for your community of faith.
+ Pray that God would continue to strengthen you in faith.

Source of Life, we give you thanks for calling us into relationship with you. We give you thanks for the gift of baptism that unites us with you and with all the baptized of the past, the present, and the future. Help us now, as we examine our common statement of faith, to proclaim with certainty, "I believe." We pray this in the name of the Holy Trinity. Amen.

DAY 18, THURSDAY

The First Article: On Creation

I believe in God, the Father almighty,
creator of heaven and earth.

WHAT IS THIS? *or* WHAT DOES THIS MEAN?

I believe that God has created me
together with all that exists.
God has given me
and still preserves my body and soul:
eyes, ears, and all limbs and senses;
reason and all mental faculties.

In addition, God daily and abundantly provides
shoes and clothing, food and drink,
house and farm, spouse and children,
fields, livestock, and all property—
along with all the necessities and nourishment
for this body and life.
God protects me against all danger
and shields and preserves me from all evil.
And all this is done out of pure, fatherly,
and divine goodness and mercy,
without any merit or worthiness of mine at all!
For all of this I owe it to God
to thank and praise, serve and obey him.
This is most certainly true. (SC)

PAUSE AND REFLECT

"I believe that God has created me. . . ." God has created you. Amid all the theories of the big bang, primordial gases, the survival of the fittest, God breaks into your life to announce to you that you are created.

Not just you, but God has also created all the millions and billions of earthlings on this spaceship earth, and the universe with its vastness and variety that is beyond all comprehension.

God is the extravagant creator who is fascinated with the infinite variety of shapes, sounds, and colours that make up each species, each planet, each solar system, and each of the multiple galaxies.

God has created you, unique in fingerprints, unique in DNA, unique in genetic structure. No other like you will pass through the universe. You are one of a kind created by this prodigal God.

For many people it is hard to grasp this wonder. Perhaps there is a skeptic in you who whispers, "This makes no sense." It may be easier to believe you are nothing but a chance selection of protein cast through the universe. Or because of family background, because of influences you have met along the journey, you may feel you are not worth much.

The book of Genesis, however, says that as each part of the world unfolded under the creative hand of God, God said, "This is good." God had an intention for all that was created, and it was good. *You* are created for this good. There is plan and purpose and destiny in your creation. You have been placed here for good and for God. Nothing can shake away that plan or that hope for you.

The Bible is very clear about this:

> For it was you who formed my inward parts;
>   you knit me together in my mother's womb.
> I praise you, for I am fearfully and wonderfully made.
>   Wonderful are your works;
> that I know very well.
> Psalm 139:13-14

> "Before I formed you in the womb I knew you,
> and before you were born I consecrated you;
> I appointed you a prophet to the nations."
> Jeremiah 1:5

> So God created humankind in his image,
>   in the image of God he created them;
>   male and female he created them.
> Genesis 1:27

Dare to take the jump of faith and stand in awe and wonder at the prospect of being created, formed, and shaped by this creator God.

PRAY

+ Pray for people who feel they are not worth much, that they may come to know the wonder of their creation.

+ Give thanks to God for your creation.

+ Spend time considering the thought and care of God reaching to you.

+ Pray that God will give you wonder at the marvel and complexity of all creation.

+ Thank God for all of creation, especially for the things you enjoy.

Life-Giver and Source of All Being, you amaze us with the beauty and intricacy of the created world. We praise you for your love of diversity. We are awed to think that you have created us, just the way we are. Help us to love ourselves because of the great love you have for us. Empower us to love and care for one another and the earth because you have created them in love as well. We pray in your life-giving name. Amen.

DAY 19, FRIDAY

The First Article: On Creation

I believe in God, the Father almighty,
creator of heaven and earth.

WHAT IS THIS? *or* WHAT DOES THIS MEAN?

I believe that God has created me
together with all that exists.
God has given me . . . (SC)

PAUSE AND REFLECT

"I believe that God has given me . . . ," says Luther. Through these words, Luther clearly states who God is and who you are. God is the giver; you are the gift, and you receive gifts.

You may have heard of a "self-made person," someone applauded for their vigour in rising to the top. The first article of the Apostles' Creed says there is no self-made person, for everything you have is a gift.

Maybe you are tempted to say, "It is mine." If you have succeeded in something, it is easy to say, "I did it!" You may say, "I have worked hard and I have earned every penny." The creed says that God has given you gifts.

You may say, "I will go to school and take a course at the university so that I can find a good job for myself and have an easy life." God says that you are a gift and everything that you have received is a gift. In this age of privatization and emphasis on individual achievement, it is hard to hear this other word.

You will see yourself, others, and all creation in such a different way when you look at everything in the light of gift, for in this light all is seen as being connected to God. You are called, and you call others, to see the reality of this good word each time you are in church and celebrate the Lord's supper. The offerings of bread and wine and money are brought forward, and the whole congregation prays a prayer similar to this:

> Blessed are you, O God, maker of all things. Through your goodness you have bless-
> ed us with these gifts: our selves, our time, and our possessions. Use us, and what we

have gathered, in feeding the world with your love, through the one who gave himself for us, Jesus Christ, our Savior and Lord.[1]

PRAY

+ Spend the day with God, giving thanks for creation. Try to be conscious of the gifts of God throughout the day, and express your thanks.

+ Pray for those who struggle to see that they are a gift to others and to the world.

+ Pray for the church, which is a gift from God to the world.

Giver of all good things, we thank and praise you for all the gifts we have received. Our lives, our accomplishments, our possessions—all are gifts from you. Help us to be thankful for what we have been given. Enable us to generously share from these gifts to show our love for you and to help those in need around us. We pray in your generous name. Amen.

DAY 20, SATURDAY

The First Article: On Creation

I believe in God, the Father almighty,
creator of heaven and earth.

WHAT IS THIS? *or* WHAT DOES THIS MEAN?

I believe that God has created me
together with all that exists.
God has given me
and still preserves . . . (SC)

PAUSE AND REFLECT

There is a farmer who lives in Saskatchewan who has determined that the land he tills will be better when he dies than when he first started farming. I think he will succeed. Everyone in his family helps in running the farm. He uses only natural fertilizers. Sheep eat the weeds from his summer fallow, preserving precious moisture in a dry land. He is content to recycle farm machinery and has the gift to make the old work again. Turkeys have stopped a grasshopper infestation, and guinea hens and dogs keep unwanted pests away. The food of the table is great, and this farmer is content with his life. He sees himself as a partner with God in preserving the good earth for future generations and cultivating something better.

Will the earth be better cared for by the time you die? Like this farmer, you have a choice: Is the gift of the earth given to you only to use as you will, or is it also to be given to future generations?

In the state of Oaxaca in Mexico lives a man whose name is Eliab. He too has caught the vision. He has decided not to leave his impoverished farm to go to the city for a job. He feels that God has called him to preserve the land and to make it better by staying in his village.

Decisions like these bring new visions. Eliab now sees his animals and his family in the same caring way that he sees the land. He has also come to understand that he is not doing this for himself, but for all the people in the world. The trees he has planted will give oxygen to polluted cities like Mexico City, New York, and Tokyo.

He sees himself helping to preserve the land for the sake of the world. You should meet him, for he is working with you.

Then there are the words of Chief Qwatsinas of the Nuxalk Nation:

> Forests sustain life. We must keep our forests to nurture our most valuable resource, our children. We must keep our trees to provide us with oxygen. It would be suicide to deliberately extinguish all of our main oxygen supply. . . . We not only speak for ourselves, but also for the birds, trees, animals, fish, sky. . . . for the future of our children, grandchildren and children yet to be born.[2]

All of these stories speak of people who have caught a vision of God's plan for preserving the earth. Do you share this vision?

PRAY

+ Pray for those who farm, that they may share the vision.
+ Pray for those who seek to preserve wildlife, forests, and dreams.
+ Pray for those who suffer from drought and its accompanying hunger.
+ Ask God to enable you to see ways that you can preserve the earth.
+ Pray for all who work to preserve the earth.

Creating God, you have placed us on this beautiful earth and entrusted us with its use and care. We confess the harm that we have done to our planet—to the earth, to the air, and to the water. Help us to recognize the impact that our daily choices have on the earth. Strengthen our resolve to make changes to restore your creation to health. Give us your vision to care for the earth for the sake of future generations. In your life-giving name we pray. Amen.

DAY 21, SUNDAY

This is Sunday. Before you attend worship, think of the people in your parish. Who comes with great need? Whom can you greet with a word of peace? Ask God to help you to be open to newcomers and to people who are different from you.

PRAY

Holy God, we gather to worship you this day, joined with those around the world who will also confess that they believe. We lift up those around us who are in great need, and ask you to use us to respond to these needs. We remember those with whom we are in disagreement, and ask for courage to share your peace with them. We ask you to open our hearts to welcome everyone into our community of worship, especially those who are different from us. We pray these things in your holy name. Amen.

DAY 22, MONDAY

The Second Article: On Redemption

I believe in Jesus Christ, God's only Son, our Lord,
who was conceived by the Holy Spirit,
born of the virgin Mary,
suffered under Pontius Pilate,
was crucified, died, and was buried;
he descended to the dead.
On the third day he rose again;
he ascended into heaven,
he is seated at the right hand of the Father,
and he will come to judge the living and the dead.

WHAT IS THIS? *or* WHAT DOES THIS MEAN?

I believe that Jesus Christ, true God,
begotten of the Father in eternity,
and also a true human being,
born of the virgin Mary,
is my Lord.
He has redeemed me,
a lost and condemned human being.
He has purchased and freed me from all sins,
from death, and from the power of the devil,
not with gold or silver
but with his holy, precious blood
and with his innocent suffering and death.
He has done all this
in order that I may belong to him,
live under him in his kingdom,
and serve him in eternal righteousness, innocence,
and blessedness,
just as he is risen from the dead

and lives and rules eternally.
This is most certainly true. (SC)

PAUSE AND REFLECT

Jesus Christ has freed you from sin, death, and the power of the devil. A prayer that can be used before holy communion puts it this way:

> We give you thanks, Father, through Jesus Christ, your beloved Son, whom you sent in this end of the ages to save and redeem us and to proclaim to us your will. . . .

> He, our Lord Jesus, fulfilled all your will and won for you a holy people; he stretched out his hands in suffering in order to free from suffering those who trust you.

> He is the one who, handed over to a death he freely accepted, in order to destroy death, to break the bonds of the evil one, to crush hell underfoot, to give light to the righteous, to establish his covenant, and to show forth the resurrection, taking bread and giving thanks to you, said: Take and eat, this is my body, given for you.[3]

You may not realize it right now, but this action of Christ in destroying the power of death, sin, hell, and the evil one was *for you.* The power of sin to destroy and condemn you is broken. The power of death to make you fear the future is vanquished. Hell has no claim on you because you bear the name of Christ. All evil, with its power to capture and destroy, has been shown to be toothless and will not win the age.

All of this is given to you as a gift. You are invited to believe that this is so, and to live your life freed from this power.

This does not mean that you will not experience pain or loss or death. But it is a promise that pain and loss and death will not have the final word. God is with you at all times and will have the final word for your life.

You may be one who carries, like a ball and chain, the burden of past mistakes. You are invited to let go of these; knowing that in Christ there is forgiveness.

You may be one caught up in actions that appear to bring only destruction. In Christ you can be transformed.

You may fear the future, fear the evil that surrounds you, fear the grip that evil has on the world. The future does not belong to evil, but to Christ and to you.

You may fear death. You may fear death for those you love—your children, your parents, your partner—as well as for yourself. The resurrection of Christ is a sign that death has no power over his people. Even at the time of death the One who is the resurrection and the life will be with you.

PRAY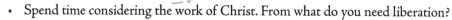

materialism — complacency — worry

+ Spend time considering the work of Christ. From what do you need liberation?

+ Pray for those preparing to be baptized, that they may live freely in the faith.

+ Pray for those who are dying, that they may know the comfort of the gospel.

+ Pray for those who grieve, that they may be comforted by God's presence and promises. *Ukraine*

Liberating God, we give you thanks and praise for the freedom you have given us. We give you thanks for our salvation. We give you thanks for your presence with us in the hard times of our lives. We pray that the freedom we have in you will give us courage to reach out to those who are suffering and to challenge those who are causing harm. In Jesus' name we pray. Amen.

DAY 23, TUESDAY

The Second Article: On Redemption

He has purchased and freed me from all sins,
from death, and from the power of the devil,
not with gold or silver
but with his holy, precious blood
and with his innocent suffering and death. (SC)

PAUSE AND REFLECT

Before God brought the Israelites out of slavery in Egypt, they were saved from death by marking their doorposts with lambs' blood. During Passover, Jewish communities continue to remember how God saved the people.

The cross of Christ is now the mark of your salvation. The cross was a cruel instrument of torture and death for runaway slaves, criminals, and subversives throughout the Roman Empire. It has become the centre of the Christian faith, for it is here that God's presence was made known most intimately. It is here in the vulnerability, the weakness, the suffering, the loneliness, and the dying that God comes.

You may have thought that God should come and be known in holiness, in splendour, in riches, in wondrous miracles, in universal truth, in high moral standards. You may have looked for God here. God is present in all these. But it is in the vulnerability of death on the cross that God is most visible.

God has entered our pain, our vulnerability, our loneliness, our weakness, in order to touch us and save us. There is no pain so great, no loneliness so vast, no vulnerability so low, and no weakness so extensive that it will escape God's presence.

You are invited to place yourself before this cross of death. You are invited to come and bring with you the pain of your life and of others. Christ has entered that pain. You too may be moved like the writer of the hymn "Ah, holy Jesus":

> For me, kind Jesus, was thine incarnation,
> thy mortal sorrow, and thy life's oblation;
> thy death of anguish and thy bitter passion,
> for my salvation.

Therefore, kind Jesus, since I cannot pay thee,
I do adore thee, and will ever pray thee;
think on thy pity and thy love unswerving,
not my deserving.[4]

PRAY

+ Ask God to give you strength in facing evil and death.

+ Pray for the courage to call out evil when you see it.

+ Give thanks to God for the love shown in Jesus' death on the cross.

+ Spend time in silence. In your imagination, stand before the cross and give thanks.

God our saviour, we give you thanks for Jesus, who came into our world to live as one of us. We give you thanks for his willingness to stand in the face of evil and to face death on a cross. In his defeat of death, we have our salvation.

Merciful God, you wrap your arms around us in times of vulnerability, loneliness, and weakness. Help us to feel your presence with us and to take comfort and strength from your endless love. Guide us to share that love with others in their pain. In your tender name we pray. Amen.

DAY 24, WEDNESDAY

The Second Article: On Redemption

He has done all this
in order that I may belong to him,
live under him in his kingdom,
and serve him in eternal righteousness, innocence,
and blessedness,
just as he is risen from the dead
and lives and rules eternally.
This is most certainly true. (SC)

PAUSE AND REFLECT

"Child of God, you have been sealed by the Holy Spirit and marked with the cross of Christ forever."[5] Through baptism you are a member of the body of Christ. You bear on your forehead the seal of your belonging. First Peter 2:10 puts it this way: "Once you were not a people, but now you are God's people."

You are part of a family that stretches back beyond Abraham and Sarah, to whom God promised to give land and many descendants. You are a member of a family that looks into the future with optimism. You are adopted into the household of faith. You belong to God. You may have neglected this for many years of your life. This covenant, however, remains true, and you are invited to be renewed in it every day.

Martin Luther suggests that you are to be renewed each morning. He said that when you get out of bed and your feet hit the floor, make the sign of the cross on your forehead and remember that you are a child of God.

As God's child, you live under God and the reign of God. This reign of peace and justice; this reign of forgiveness and reconciliation; this reign that knows no walls between rich and poor, between genders, between races, between differing abilities—this reign is not something for which we wait. Some say that the reign of God is only a future reality, "pie in the sky when you die, by and by." Not so. This is a present reality. You are called to be a sign of God's reign each day of your life.

You, along with the whole body of Christ, witness to the coming rule of God. Sometimes you will fail at this, other times you will be faithful, but it is the here and now in which God's rule begins. Today, and each day, you are a witness to God's gracious rule.

For today, consider ways in which you are called to be part of God's reign in your family, your work, your church, and your community. You go out each day as a forgiven person. This should give you courage to take risks, to make mistakes, to be a child of the reign of God.

And as Luther writes at the end of each of his meditations on the Apostles' Creed: "This is most certainly true."

PRAY

+ Ask God to help you this day.
+ Thank God for the promise that you belong to God.
+ Pray for your pastor and other leaders in your parish.

Loving God, you bring us into one family on earth and beyond time. You love us all equally and call us to work in and for your reign of justice and peace, forgiveness and reconciliation. Help us to joyfully work together to fulfill your desire for this present and future reality. We pray with open and thankful hearts. Amen.

DAY 25, THURSDAY

The Third Article: On Being Made Holy

I believe in the Holy Spirit,
the holy catholic church,
the communion of saints,
the forgiveness of sins,
the resurrection of the body,
and the life everlasting. Amen.

WHAT IS THIS? *or* WHAT DOES THIS MEAN?

I believe that by my own understanding or strength
I cannot believe in Jesus Christ my Lord
or come to him,
but instead the Holy Spirit
has called me through the gospel,
enlightened me with his gifts, made me holy
and kept me in the true faith,
just as he calls, gathers, enlightens, and makes holy
the whole Christian church on earth
and keeps it with Jesus Christ
in the one common, true faith.
Daily in this Christian church
the Holy Spirit abundantly forgives all sins—
mine and those of all believers.
On the last day the Holy Spirit will raise me
and all the dead
and will give to me and all believers in Christ
eternal life.
This is most certainly true. (SC)

PAUSE AND REFLECT

Now we turn our attention to the work of the Holy Spirit, this gentle one of the Trinity, this soft breeze that woos us and stirs faith in us.

This is the same Spirit who was present in creation and moved over the face of the waters. This is the same Spirit who is the breath of life that has been breathed into us. This is the same Spirit who was present at the call of Abraham and Sarah, Moses and Miriam, all of the prophets, and all the people of Israel as they were called forth into life.

This is the same Spirit who came to Mary and called forth the life of Jesus in her body. This is the same Spirit Jesus gave to his disciples when he breathed on them and said, "Receive the Holy Spirit." This is the same Spirit who was made known to the church at Pentecost. This is the same Spirit who has been at work in you and is given to you in baptism.

This is the same Spirit who calls you this day to follow the way of our Lord. This is the same Spirit who gives the gifts of peace, hope, joy, love, patience, kindness, generosity, faithfulness, gentleness, and self-control. This is the same Spirit who is the gift to the people of God for the ministry of the church.

Within us there is always that ego that wants to proclaim, "Look what I have found, look what I have discovered, look what I have done, look what I deserve." But we know that is not true. This faith, this covenant, this ability to be open to God is all gift.

This quiet, unassuming Spirit of God comes in gentleness but is also filled with strength. It is this Spirit who gave courage to martyrs as they proclaimed the faith. It is this Spirit who calls for workers for justice and peace like Medardo Gómez, bishop of the Lutheran Church in El Salvador and Nobel Peace Prize nominee. It is this Spirit who gives inner power to us to withstand temptation. It is this Spirit who binds people together in congregations and churches, and binds together the whole Christian church on earth.

This Spirit has no shape or form that we know. The Spirit comes to us dressed as a dove, as the wind, and in the shape of fire. The Spirit has come to us and will come to others as pastors speak the words in the baptismal service, "Receive the Spirit." And the Spirit is always present, calling, gathering, and working for the reign of God.

PRAY

+ Thank God for the gift of the Spirit and the gift of faith.
+ Pray that the will of the Spirit is created in you.
+ Pray that you would be able to see the Spirit working in those around you.
+ Pray that we will come to see the gifts of the Spirit in us, gifts that will strengthen the work of the church in its mission.

Creating and renewing God, we give you thanks for the gift of the Holy Spirit. We pray that we would see the Spirit's work in those around us and in all of creation. Strengthen your Spirit within us, that we may be led to use the gifts that you have given us for the sake of the world you love so much. In the name of the Holy Spirit we pray. Amen.

DAY 26, FRIDAY

The Third Article: On Being Made Holy

I believe in . . . the holy catholic church,
the communion of saints . . . (SC)

PAUSE AND REFLECT

There is diversity in the catholic (universal) church: Presbyterians, Methodists, Pentecostals, Baptists, Mennonites, Disciples, Anglicans, Episcopalians, Congregationalists, Roman Catholics, Adventists, Lutherans, Friends, and Covenanters; United Church, Orthodox, and Christian Reformed believers; and many more. These groups and denominations meet in chapels, homes, cathedrals, open fields, caves, storefront missions, hospitals, prisons, shelters, stadiums, theatres, and every variety of rented quarters from bars to funeral homes. During the pandemic, some have gathered outdoors. Others have come together online. Each group or denomination also has its own history, traditions, and way of worshiping.

There is unity in the catholic church too. While the many groups and denominations have different meeting places, histories, traditions, and worship practices, they all confess the same Lord.

This unity in Christ extends even further. The one body of the holy catholic church lives in communion with *all* who are connected to Christ: to our forebears in the faith, the Jews; to all those who have died in Christ; to the whole company of heaven; and to all people who will be baptized into Christ's body in the future. When we gather to celebrate the Lord's supper, we celebrate that our table is connected to angels and archangels, to all the company of heaven, and to all the company on earth.

The congregation to which you belong is important, for this is where Christ takes on flesh for you in this time. The Spirit of God binds you in this faith community to the church catholic that extends beyond space and time.

PRAY

+ Give thanks for the Spirit who holds us together in the body of Christ.
+ Give thanks for church leaders, bishops, pastors, and deacons of all denominations.

- Pray that God will raise up people to work and serve in the church in various ways.
- Pray for the unity of the church, and for the Spirit to remove all barriers that divide us.
- Pray for your own parish, for all the people, for the newly baptized, for all who offer themselves to serve on boards and committees.
- Pray for all who teach and lead in the church, that they may be strengthened in ministry and drawn together in unity.

Holy God, you call us to be part of your holy church. Bind us not just to our congregation and our denomination, but to the faithful around the world, to the saints who have gone before us, and to all the baptized who will follow. We confess that we sometimes act in unholy ways and harm the body of Christ. Send your Holy Spirit to lead and guide and strengthen us to be faithful followers of you. Raise up among us faithful leaders, equip them with the skills they need, and help us to support them in their work. We pray all these things in your most holy name. Amen.

DAY 27, SATURDAY

The Third Article: On Being Made Holy

I believe in . . . the forgiveness of sins. . . .

WHAT IS THIS? *or* WHAT DOES THIS MEAN?

Daily in this Christian church
the Holy Spirit abundantly forgives all sins—
mine and those of all believers. (SC)

PAUSE AND REFLECT

Consider the generosity of God. Each sin in your life is forgiven. You stand in relationship to God through baptism, and this relationship assures you of the forgiveness of all your sins.

Why then would you go through days, weeks, months, and sometimes years hanging on to guilt? Guilt is a destructive force. It can cause you to hide from God and others, afraid of exposure and dreading the judgment that God and others may place upon you.

God wants you to know that there is forgiveness for you each day. When your sins trouble you, the Spirit invites you to confess and be assured that you are forgiven.

This may be hard to hear, and hard to take to heart. You may need the help of a pastor or friend to see that this forgiveness is yours. But be sure of this: living with unresolved guilt is not God's intent for you. Therefore, God offers forgiveness day by day.

To stand in the wonderful light of forgiveness permits new life and new possibilities to flood into your life. This is like the newness you feel when you take a shower after a long, hard day of physical toil. It is like the newness of a fresh spring morning. It is a resurrection from an old life to new life.

Jesus healed many people during his ministry. When he saw a man who had been ill and unable to walk for many years, he told the man, "Stand up, take your mat and walk" (John 5:8). Jesus extends this invitation to you each day: *Rise and walk in newness of life.* This is the way of God, to lift up the fallen, to raise up those who are low. It is a part of the resurrection of Christ. It is a lifelong journey.

When you are baptized, you receive the robe of righteousness—not your own righteousness, but the righteousness of Christ. It is a garment that is way too big for you, like a hand-me-down from a beloved older sibling. You spend your whole life trying to grow into it, but God always looks at you, sees you wearing the righteousness of Christ, and continues to forgive you.

PRAY

+ Pray that God will help you to see others, knowing that their sins are also forgiven.

+ If you bear guilt from things in the past, ask God for release from this guilt or talk with your pastor about this.

+ Thank God for the abundant forgiveness that awaits you each day.

Loving God, we thank you for placing on us Christ's robes of righteousness. Guide us to wear these garments in ways that will honour and serve you. Forgive us when we sin and fall short of Christ's example. Help us to receive your forgiveness not just in our heads, but also in our hearts. Lead us to look on those around us and remember that they too are forgiven and wearing the same robes of righteousness. Help us to grow in faith and love towards you. In the name of Jesus we pray. Amen.

DAY 28, SUNDAY

This is Sunday. Pray for all those preparing for baptism or affirmation of baptism. Pray also for the young people in your parish, and in confirmation class, who are on the journey. Be open to them and welcome them.

Prepare for worship by praying for all those who bring their gifts to the community in worship. Pray that your parish may be open and hospitable to those who come seeking.

PRAY

Jesus our brother, we thank you for sharing with us your robes of righteousness. We thank you for our siblings in Christ who will gather to worship around the world today. Help us to look on one another with your loving eyes and to see others as your beloved, forgiven, and holy children. Open our hearts to receive your blessings this day through our common worship. We pray in your holy name. Amen.

DAY 29, MONDAY

The Third Article: On Being Made Holy

I believe in . . . the resurrection of the body,
and the life everlasting . . . (SC)

PAUSE AND REFLECT

The song "I Was There to Hear Your Borning Cry" by John C. Ylvisaker is sung by God to you.

> I was there to hear your borning cry,
> I'll be there when you are old.
> I rejoiced the day you were baptized,
> To see your life unfold.

The song touches on teenage rebellion, marriage, middle years, and then concludes:

> When the evening gently closes in
> and you shut your weary eyes,
> I'll be there as I have always been
> with just one more surprise.[6]

Just one more surprise. Being baptized into Christ is also to be baptized into the resurrection. Death follows you on your journey, but because of Christ, you know that death has no real power. For even as Christ is risen from the dead and lives forever, so it is for all who are in Christ.

Death means the loss of people and things important to you. You will bury loved ones in sorrow. But besides the sorrow, you can bury your loved ones in hope, for Christ's victory over death and the grave belongs to all the people of God.

On Ash Wednesday the pastor makes the sign of the cross on your brow, accompanied by these words: "Remember that you are dust, and to dust you shall return." This is true, for death is ever-present. Its reality is inevitable. It is the way of the created order. No matter what you may do to hide from this fact, it is true for you.

Ash Wednesday is the beginning of a journey that takes us to Easter and beyond. On Easter you hear of the Lord's resurrection, and the hope of new life for all the people of God.

PRAY

+ Pray for those who are dying, that they may receive God's comfort.

+ Pray for those who mourn the loss of loved ones.

+ Consider your own death. Does this bring fear, anxiety, regret? Place this over against the words of the Apostles' Creed, and thank God for the resurrection from the dead.

God of life and death, we praise you for the resurrection hope we have in Christ, for our loved ones and for ourselves. Teach us not to fear death, and to rely on your promises of life eternal. Remind us when we mourn that you are with us and have promised to turn our mourning into joy and our sorrow into gladness (Jeremiah 31:13). We pray in the name of your resurrected Son, Jesus the Christ. Amen.

DAY 30, TUESDAY

The Third Article: On Being Made Holy

I believe in . . . the resurrection of the body,
and the life everlasting . . . (SC)

PAUSE AND REFLECT

During the past few days you have been reflecting on the Apostles' Creed. This is one of the creeds recognized by the Christian church as a strong statement of faith. It is the creed used at your baptism, and it will be used at your death.

You will have many opportunities in your worship life to say this creed. Spend some time today looking back over the past several days. Consider some ways in which the Apostles' Creed has affected you.

Consider the work of creation. Such wonder fills the earth! Each day there is something new for you to see, hear, touch, taste, and smell in this creation. You too are a part of the wonder of this creation.

Consider the work of salvation. God through Jesus the Christ has revealed such love and compassion for you and for the whole world. It is for you that the Christ has come to bring life. It is for you that he laid down his life. It is for you and for the whole world that God raised Jesus from death, that you might live in the promise of the resurrection.

Consider the Spirit who has called you into a community and even now to this time of prayer. This Spirit will lead and guide you into the joy and fullness of the reign of God.

"In the name of the Father, and of the Son, and of the Holy Spirit," or a similar phrase, is announced at baptisms and each time the community of faith gathers. In the Apostles' Creed we confess our faith in this triune God.

PRAY

+ Give thanks to God for this understanding of God.
+ Pray for all those who will be baptized, that their love of God may grow.

+ Pray for the whole church, that it may be strengthened in this wonderful mystery of the Trinity.

Triune God, we give you thanks and praise for your creating, redeeming, and regenerative work among us and all creation. Help us to remember each day the words used at baptism that recount your holy name, Three-in-One and One-in-Three. Be with us as we continue to divine this holy mystery that issues both life and new life. We pray in your holy name. Amen.

TEACH US
TO PRAY ...
The Lord's Prayer

DAY 31, WEDNESDAY

Our Father in heaven,
hallowed be your name,
your kingdom come,
your will be done, on earth as in heaven.
Give us today our daily bread.
Forgive us our sins
as we forgive those who sin against us.
Save us from the time of trial
and deliver us from evil.
For the kingdom, the power, and the glory are yours,
now and forever. Amen. (SC)

[Jesus] was praying in a certain place, and after he
had finished, one of his disciples said to him, "Lord,
teach us to pray, as John taught his disciples."

Luke 11:1

PAUSE AND REFLECT

During the past weeks you have prayed through the ten commandments, looking at the question of "no other gods." The Apostles' Creed followed, and you explored what you believe and the faith of the church in the God revealed. Now you who prepare for baptism, and you who prepare for the service of Affirmation of Baptism, along with the whole community of God, ask Jesus as the disciples did: "Teach us to pray."

Prayer is at the heart of Christian spirituality. The scriptures invite us to "pray without ceasing" (1 Thessalonians 5:17). We are encouraged to "pray for one another" (James 5:16). We are invited to "let [our] requests be made known to God" (Philippians 4:6). The parables of Jesus on the topic of prayer inform us that God listens attentively, as a good parent.

During these past weeks you have been invited to pray every day, and to join the community in prayer each Sunday. What has this experience taught you about prayer? Spend some time reflecting on this experience.

Prayer takes time. Do you have the time? There needs to be time to focus, to listen, and to speak. Prayer involves as much listening as it does speaking. There is nothing more boring than a one-way conversation.

What space allows you to listen and speak as you pray? You can use any number of spaces in your home, in a church, outdoors as you walk, and so on. Some people use a candle, an altar, the Bible, or a painting to begin their time of prayer, to call them away from their busy lives, and to focus on conversation with God.

PRAY

+ Spend some time being in the presence of God without words. With God you are already connected to all that you need.

Holy God, come into this time and place now and be with us. Help us to be aware of your presence, to feel you with us as we breathe in and breathe out. Open our ears, our hearts, and our minds to listen for your presence and to hear your word to us. Amen.

DAY 32, THURSDAY

Introduction

Our Father in heaven.

WHAT IS THIS? *or* WHAT DOES THIS MEAN?

With these words God wants to attract us,
so that we come to believe he is truly our Father
and we are truly his children,
in order that we may ask him boldly
and with complete confidence,
just as loving children ask their loving father. (SC)

PAUSE AND REFLECT

"Our Father." How far does *our* go for you? Does it only include your family? Does it include your church? Does it extend to the neighbourhood, to the city, or even to the nation? Does it include all people in the nation, or just the Lutherans, just the Christians, just a certain political party, just a certain group with common values? Does it extend to other nations, to other races and cultures, to people of differing economic status, sexual orientation, or gender? Does it include those who upheld apartheid in South Africa, conspiracy theorists, hard-core racists, gang members, drug dealers? Keep in mind that God is always trying to expand the inclusiveness of our prayers.

Abba (which means "Father" in Aramaic) is an intimate, familiar term. Jesus invites us to remember the God of intimacy and to use this term when we pray. Can God be that close and intimate?

Listen to God speak in Isaiah:

Zion said, "The LORD has forsaken me,
my Lord has forgotten me."
Can a woman forget her nursing child,
or show no compassion for the child of her womb?
Even these may forget,
yet I will not forget you.
Isaiah 49:14-15

Or listen to the psalmist:

> As a father has compassion for his children,
>   so the LORD has compassion for those who fear him.
> For he knows how we were made;
>   he remembers that we are dust.
> Psalm 103:13-14

Listen also to the word of God from Deuteronomy 32:11-12a:

> As an eagle stirs up its nest,
>   and hovers over its young;
> as it spreads its wings, takes them up,
>   and bears them aloft on its pinions,
> the LORD alone guided [his people].

As Jesus teaches his disciples to pray, he reminds them of the caring and intimacy that God extends to them and to you. Think of endearing words that you use with someone who is your beloved—a spouse, parent, child, or dear friend. If possible use these words as you talk to God.

PRAY

+ Pray for those who prepare for baptism.

+ Pray for those who do not know God or whose only prayer is a cry for help.

+ Imagine you are a young eagle in the nest and your mother is watching over you. What do you have to say to her? Can you say the same things to God?

Abba, you are love divine, and you call us into a relationship of intimacy. Yet it is hard for us to feel close to one who is so holy and majestic. Open our hearts to receive and experience your deep love for us and to relax into your strong, loving arms. Help us to love you in return with total trust and openness. Remind us that your love extends to all your creation, even those we want to label as "other." Amen.

DAY 33, FRIDAY

The First Petition

Hallowed be your name.

WHAT IS THIS? *or* WHAT DOES THIS MEAN?

It is true that God's name is holy in itself,
but we ask in this prayer
that it may also become holy in and among us.

HOW DOES THIS COME ABOUT?

Whenever the word of God
is taught clearly and purely
and we, as God's children,
also live holy lives according to it.
To this end help us, dear Father in heaven!
However, whoever teaches and lives
otherwise than the word of God teaches,
dishonors the name of God among us.
Preserve us from this, heavenly Father! (SC)

PAUSE AND REFLECT

The writers of scripture name or describe God with these words and more: Yahweh (Jehovah), Adonai (Lord), I AM WHO I AM, Creator, Sustainer, Father, Mother, Preserver, Spirit, Son of God, Jesus the Christ, vine, vinedresser, mother eagle, fortress, Saviour, almighty, Sophia (Wisdom), rock, mother hen, nursing mother, gardener, shepherd, pregnant woman, judge, ruler, bread of life, water of life, Lamb of God, Deliverer, Redeemer, LORD of Hosts, strong right arm in battle, lion, Son of Man.

Which of these names are important for you? Can you think of other names or descriptions of God? Which of these names do you use in your conversation with others about God? Which do you hear used in worship, preaching, and hymns?

For many people, Father (Abba) is the most common name for God. That is the name Jesus used when he taught us to pray. But for some people, the image of father

86

is a difficult one, especially when there has been abuse by a male parent or male role model. We need to respect all the names of God, and the needs of our siblings among us, by being open to using more than one name for God.

PRAY

+ Pray that we may keep God's name holy among us.

+ Pray that we will proclaim and use many of God's names.

+ Pray for your congregation as it worships.

+ Pray for all who hunger for God, but for whom the church is a stumbling block.

God, you are so big that no one name can contain you. You are a multifaceted jewel. Help us to love and honour you in the way we use your names. Keep us from making any one name an idol to limit or control you. In all of your holy names we pray. Amen.

DAY 34, SATURDAY

The Second Petition

Your kingdom come.

WHAT IS THIS? *or* WHAT DOES THIS MEAN?

In fact, God's kingdom comes on its own
without our prayer,
but we ask in this prayer
that it may also come to us.

HOW DOES THIS COME ABOUT?

Whenever our heavenly Father
gives us his Holy Spirit,
so that through the Holy Spirit's grace
we believe God's holy word
and live godly lives here in time
and hereafter in eternity. (SC)

PAUSE AND REFLECT

The rule of God comes among us to break down the walls of division that we establish—walls between races, between genders, between people of differing economic status, between people of varying abilities, between old and young, Indigenous and settler, labour and management, healthy and ill. You may be able to add to this list.

When God's rule finally comes over the earth, all these barriers that we have established will be gone. As you pray this petition in the Lord's Prayer, you are asking for grace to see this future reality as a present reality, and inviting God to help you live as an agent of reconciliation in today's world.

A hymn from the 1983 World Council of Churches meeting in Vancouver eloquently expresses this hope and this reality:

Walls that divide are broken down,
Christ is our unity.
Chains that enslave are thrown aside,
Christ is our liberty.[1]

Scripture speaks of a time when "righteousness and peace will kiss each other" (Psalm 85:10). As the church prays and works for justice and peace, the reign of God is illumined for all to see.

PRAY

+ Ask God to give you grace to see the walls that you have created.

+ Pray that you may be an agent of God's reconciliation.

+ Pray for the nation and its leaders, that God would stir up a hunger for justice and peace.

God of justice and peace, give us a vision of the reign that you would establish. Help us to work to break down barriers that keep us from one another. Empower us to live into your rule of equity and justice. In your just and holy name we pray. Amen.

DAY 35, SUNDAY

This is Sunday. Pray for all the bishops in your church. Many will preach this Sunday and need your gift of prayer. Pray for your pastor, for church musicians, for worship assistants. Pray for help in listening and responding to God's word proclaimed this day. Pray for those who are unable to be present in the community due to health, work, travel, and other reasons.

PRAY

God of many names, All-Holy One, as we gather to worship you this day, keep our eyes and ears open to hear and honour your varied and splendid names. As we pray and sing and listen and wait in silent anticipation, be with us and unite us with those around us and with all of your beloved around the world. Help us to see signs of your reign in our communities and in one another. Amen.

DAY 36, MONDAY

The Third Petition

Your will be done, on earth as in heaven.

WHAT IS THIS? *or* WHAT DOES THIS MEAN?

In fact, God's good and gracious will
comes about without our prayer,
but we ask in this prayer
that it may also come about in and among us.

HOW DOES THIS COME ABOUT?

Whenever God breaks and hinders
every evil scheme and will—
as are present in the will of the devil, the world,
and our flesh—
that would not allow us to hallow God's name
and would prevent the coming of his kingdom,
and instead whenever God strengthens us
and keeps us steadfast in his word and in faith
until the end of our lives.
This is God's gracious and good will. (SC)

PAUSE AND REFLECT

Have you ever wished that God would take strong, powerful action to clean up the mess we and all people of the world have made? Instead God has chosen to call, to woo, and to show love and forgiveness, that the reign of God would come from the hearts of the people of the earth. God appears to have time, while we grow impatient in our hunger for the will of God.

You are one who has heard the gentle voice of God calling you to live the reign of God, to be part of God's plan of winning over the world. God invites you to pray with word and deed, "Your will be done."

How will you respond to this call?

PRAY

+ Pray for grace to see how God has called you.

+ Pray for help to see that your life is a gift to the reign of God.

+ Pray for those preparing to be baptized, that they may receive help and courage from your parish as they are called to be a part of God's will on earth.

God, we declare you our Sovereign, but we admit that we want to rule ourselves: not your will be done but our will be done . . . my will be done. Give us patience and grace to follow your call and carry out your will. Help us to let you be God so that we can be your loving followers. In your holy and majestic name we pray. Amen.

DAY 37, TUESDAY

The Fourth Petition

Give us today our daily bread.

WHAT IS THIS? *or* WHAT DOES THIS MEAN?

In fact, God gives daily bread without our prayer,
even to all evil people,
but we ask in this prayer that God cause us
to recognize what our daily bread is
and to receive it with thanksgiving.

WHAT THEN DOES "DAILY BREAD" MEAN?

Everything included in the necessities
and nourishment for our bodies,
such as food, drink, clothing, shoes,
house, farm, fields, livestock, money, property,
an upright spouse, upright children,
upright members of the household,
upright and faithful rulers, good government,
good weather, peace, health, decency, honor,
good friends, faithful neighbors, and the like. (SC)

PAUSE AND REFLECT

Give us today the bread for the day.

In images of the earth taken from space, there are no borders between countries. We are together in a spaceship called earth, and it produces enough food for its entire population to be fed.

God has promised that there will be bread for each day. This is a gift to all people. This daily bread and everything that it implies is part of the gift and grace of God.

This gift is acknowledged as we give thanks for daily bread. In Jewish homes in Jesus' time, bread was blessed and broken from a common loaf at each meal. What could you do in your home as a reminder that daily bread is a gift?

Further, daily bread is a gift to be shared. The manna God gave to the Israelites in the wilderness was to be shared with those who did not gather enough.

Yet we know that many people go without their share of daily bread. Throughout the world, 690 million people are hungry. In Canada today, one in six children under the age of eighteen is food-insecure. What about their daily bread? How can we share the bread of our tables with others?

PRAY

+ Give thanks for all that supports and sustains your life.

+ Pray for those who are hungry in your country and in countries of famine.

+ Pray for those who are unemployed and for their families as they eat the bread of the day.

+ Pray for governments to address hunger in their own countries and in the world.

+ Pray for researchers and leaders looking for solutions to the climate crisis to ensure adequate food supply for the future.

+ Pray for individuals to have open, generous hearts to share their daily bread with agencies and organizations addressing hunger.

Loving God, you provide enough daily bread for all your beloved children. But due to unfair economic practices, natural disasters, hoarding, and waste, not all of your children have enough to eat. Help us to be satisfied with our daily bread and to work for equitable sharing of food for all. Give us trust in your ongoing provision. In your generous and providential name we pray. Amen.

DAY 38, WEDNESDAY

The Fifth Petition

Forgive us our sins,
as we forgive those who sin against us.

WHAT IS THIS? *or* WHAT DOES THIS MEAN?

We ask in this prayer
that our heavenly Father would not regard our sins
nor deny these petitions on their account,
for we are worthy of nothing for which we ask,
nor have we earned it.
Instead we ask that God
would give us all things by grace,
for we sin daily
and indeed deserve only punishment.
So, on the other hand,
we, too, truly want to forgive heartily
and to do good gladly to those who sin against us.
(SC)

PAUSE AND REFLECT

This fifth petition of the Lord's Prayer may sound like a contract: Forgive others and then you will be forgiven. This is not a contract, however; it is a gracious invitation for each of us to bask in the forgiveness of God, and to be as generous with others in forgiving.

Forgiveness is not easy. How many times have you heard or said something like "I will never forgive that drunk driver"; "I will never forgive my brother who cheated me out of my inheritance"; "I will never forgive my neighbour for what she has done to me"; "I can never forgive my friend who betrayed me"; I can never forgive myself for hurting/cheating/lying/betraying . . ."? Forgiveness is hard.

Forgiveness is hard for God as well. Jesus went through the horrible death of a common criminal as he sought to announce God's reign of forgiveness. It is hard to forgive enemies. It is hard sometimes to forgive family and friends. It is often hardest of all to forgive ourselves. Jesus knows full well that it is hard, and this is why he teaches us to pray, "Forgive us our sins as we forgive those who sin against us."

PRAY

+ Remember all the times that people have forgiven you. They have been most generous when you made mistakes.

+ Do you have a long-standing fight with someone in your life? Ask God to help you forgive this person.

+ Thank God for those people who have helped you in the bond of love in spite of hurt.

+ Pray for members of your family, for members of the parish, and for members of your community, that God would lead all into ways of forgiveness.

God of bountiful forgiveness, you love us and continue to forgive us despite our repeated sins. Help us to be as generous with forgiveness with others, and to forgive ourselves, remembering that you have forgiven us. Soften our hearts. Teach us not to keep score. Let our forgiveness be genuine, not grudging or half-hearted. We pray in the name of your generous and forgiving Spirit. Amen.

DAY 39, THURSDAY

The Sixth Petition

Save us from the time of trial.

WHAT IS THIS? *or* WHAT DOES THIS MEAN?

It is true that God tempts no one,
but we ask in this prayer
that God would preserve and keep us,
so that the devil, the world, and our flesh
may not deceive us or mislead us into false belief,
despair, and other great and shameful sins,
and that, although we may be attacked by them,
we may finally prevail and gain the victory. (SC)

PAUSE AND REFLECT

The time of trial comes when the tragedies of life are enormous, when life makes no sense, when misfortune comes, when we can no longer believe in God. Save us from such a state. Save our children.

Save us from a time when we might face debilitating disease, bankruptcy, job loss, the end of a relationship, terminal illness, loneliness, despair, the loss of family members and friends. Save us too from times of natural disaster, famine, war.

The time of trial may come in something simple, or it may be complex, like the trials Job faced when he lost his entire family and everything he owned. We have loved dearly, and the time of trial may come when we are old enough that all our family members and friends have died. The time of trial may have widespread effects, as in a global pandemic.

In this petition of the Lord's Prayer, we pray that God would save us from the time of trial. If it does come, we pray that we will still place ourselves before God as Job did even after losing everything. We pray for help in the midst of trial to trust in God's grace.

PRAY

+ Pray for all experiencing times of trial due to illness, loss, bereavement.

+ Pray for those experiencing hunger, poverty, homelessness.

+ Give thanks that you are and will be in the presence of God through all of life's experiences.

God, you promise that nothing in all creation can separate us from your love. Help us to cling to that promise in times of trial. If at all possible, save us, spare us from times of trial. We pray this for ourselves, our families, and the whole world. We pray in the name of Jesus, who showed us your way of peace. Amen.

DAY 40, FRIDAY

The Seventh Petition

And deliver us from evil.

WHAT IS THIS? *or* WHAT DOES THIS MEAN?

We ask in this prayer, as in a summary,
that our Father in heaven may deliver us
from all kinds of evil—
affecting body or soul, property or reputation—
and at last, when our final hour comes,
may grant us a blessed end
and take us by grace from this valley of tears
to himself in heaven. (SC)

PAUSE AND REFLECT

Maybe you were a person who dared to believe that life is like a Norman Rockwell painting—mild, gentle, and loving. Perhaps you long for a return to that Rockwell dream, but cannot go back because you have learned that evil is more persistent and pervasive than you once imagined.

The truth is that evil is around us in many forms. It is in the marketplace that seeks to capture you and others in its addictive web. Evil is present in places plagued by abuse, racism, greed, corruption, treachery, and violence. Evil is afoot in the world and it breaks out as tyrants wage war in order to maintain power and control.

So we pray, Deliver us from evil. We ask the One who is more powerful than evil and sin to be with us, our neighbourhoods, our cities, our nation, and the world to deliver us from evil's threat.

Evil will not have the last word. The apostle Paul, considering the covenant of baptism, dared to write to the Romans: "I am convinced that neither death, nor life, nor angels, nor rulers, nor things present, nor things to come, nor powers, nor height, nor depth, nor anything else in all creation, will be able to separate us from the love of God in Christ Jesus our Lord" (Romans 8:38-39).

PRAY

- Thank God for defending you from evil, and ask for courage to know that life and mercy will prevail.

- Consider that Christ entered into the heart of evil at the time of his arrest and death. It appeared that evil had won the day, but Jesus was raised from the dead three days later. Pray that God will help you to remember this as you face evil in the world.

- Pray for those who will "renounce all the forces of evil, the devil, and all his empty promises" when they are baptized. Name them before God. Pray that they might have courage to face evil.

- Pray for individuals and families facing difficulties because of evil things they have experienced.

- Pray for the church and for people persecuted for their faith.

God, we love and proclaim your goodness. And yet we know of the evil in this world. It shouts at us constantly from all forms of media: insurrection, treachery, assassination, mass killings, racism, unfettered greed, corruption. Deliver us from these and all evils. Lead us and strengthen us to emulate your goodness in all that we do. Embolden us to confront evil and speak truth to power. In your just and righteous name we pray. Amen.

DAY 41, SATURDAY

Conclusion

For the kingdom, the power, and the glory are yours,
now and forever. Amen.

WHAT IS THIS? *or* WHAT DOES THIS MEAN?

That I should be certain
that such petitions are acceptable to
and heard by our Father in heaven,
for God himself commanded us to pray like this
and has promised to hear us.
"Amen, amen" means
"Yes, yes, it is going to come about just like this." (SC)

PAUSE AND REFLECT

This concluding part of the Lord's Prayer, this doxology of praise, was not included in the original text; it was added later. But it is fitting that we close this prayer with such a song of praise.

"Amen," we say at the end. "It is so"; "Let it be so." In some churches people say "Amen" many times during worship. This is a way for people to get into the action. "Amen!" the people shout. "Let it be so!"

When you come to the table of the Lord and receive the body of Christ given for you, you are invited to say, "Amen"; "Let it be so."

You pray the Lord's Prayer alone and in your congregation. Through this prayer you are joined to many others, with many languages, around the world. This prayer daily circles the globe and you are a part of that circle. We all shout, "Amen, amen, amen! Let it be so."

You join with the community of angels and archangels and the whole company of heaven saying, "Yes, the reign, the power, and the glory are yours, God, now and forever. Amen."

PRAY

+ Pray that this beloved prayer does not become automatic or rote within you.

+ Ask that as you pray, you will feel connected to God and to the faithful around the world.

+ Pray that you can shout "Amen, it shall be so!" when you see, hear, or feel God active in the world around you.

God, you honour us by inviting us to speak to you in prayer and promising that you will listen. We give you thanks for Jesus, who taught us to pray. May we treasure these prayerful words of Jesus and savour them as they roll off our tongues. In your holy name we pray. Amen.

DAY 42, SUNDAY

Before worship today, spend some time recalling your journey through the Lord's Prayer. Be silent before God and recall ways that God has touched you in the past weeks. Give thanks to God for this journey and the ways it has affected you. Pray for all who will be baptized and for those who will affirm their baptism. Pray for them by name. Ask God to help you see those things that prevent you from leading a full life of faith, and to show you how these things might be put to death so that the things of God may flourish.

Join the community at worship and in praying the Lord's Prayer. Remember that in this action you are intimately connected to peoples and communities all around the world (past, present, and future).

PRAY

God of all ages, we rejoice in this gift of the prayer of Jesus. We rejoice that it connects us with the faithful around the world. We treasure that it connects us with those who have gone before us and those who will come after we too have died. Bless us as we join others in this prayer today. Help us not only to say the words, but to truly hear, feel, and pray them. In your loving name we pray. Amen.

BAPTISM

DAY 43, MONDAY

[Name], child of God, you have been sealed by the Holy Spirit and marked with the cross of Christ forever.[1]

PAUSE AND REFLECT

During the next few weeks, you will consider baptism and the eucharist, their implications for your life, and your call to fulfill Christ's mission in the world.

To help with this, find a blank index card or piece of heavy paper that is approximately four inches by six inches in size. In the middle of the card, write your name. Then place a cross through your name. This represents you, a servant of Christ.

In the upper left-hand corner of the card, write "family," followed by the names of your immediate family members. There may be others in your life who are so close to you that you consider them to be part of your family; write their names on the card as well. During these next few weeks you will consider all of these people and your call to serve them.

In the upper right-hand corner, write down "work." You may have more than one job, or your work may be divided into different levels of responsibility. You may be attending school. Maybe you are at home full-time raising your children or caring for an older family member, or you may be retired. Write down those things that apply to you. During the next few weeks you will be asked to consider how you may serve Christ in this area of your life.

In the lower right-hand corner, write down "community." You are involved in a church. You may also belong to a political party or offer time to a community or sports organization. Perhaps you belong to an international organization such as Amnesty International. Another way the call of Christ comes to you is through the community.

Finally, in the lower left-hand corner, write the word "environment." Write down the names of groups you belong to that are concerned for the environment, and any outdoor activities in which you participate. The covenant with God in baptism is a call to wholeness, and the environment is a part of this.

Now use this card as a bookmark for this book. We will refer to the card as your "life card." Take time each day to look at these places where you are called to live and serve, and remember them in your prayers.

PRAY

+ Offer thanks for all of the relationships represented on your life card.

God, you model relationship for us in the mystery and relationship of the Holy Trinity. We thank you for all of the relationships that you call us into, especially our relationship with you. Make your love and care for us a model for the way we relate to family, work, community, and the environment. Bind us all together in your love and grace. In your holy name we pray. Amen.

DAY 44, TUESDAY

What Is Baptism?

Baptism is not simply plain water.
Instead, it is water used according to God's command
and connected with God's word.

WHAT THEN IS THIS WORD OF GOD?

Where our Lord Jesus Christ says in Matthew 28,
"Go therefore and make disciples of all nations,
baptizing them in the name of the Father
and of the Son and of the Holy Spirit." (SC)

PAUSE AND REFLECT

The word of God attends the water of baptism and speaks to you.

This is the same word that spoke in the creation of the world: "Then God said, 'Let there be . . .' and it was so" (Genesis 1:3-30).

This is the same word given to the Israelites on Mount Sinai. It is the same word spoken through the prophets or preachers of Israel. It is the same word that was incarnate in Jesus the Christ.

This word is now addressed to you. The baptismal word is in the form of a covenant that God makes with you. The word *covenant* is important. It is not the same as a contract. A contract says, "If you do this, then I will do this" or "If you are good, then I will keep you as a child" or "If you pray every day, then I will bless you." When God speaks to us, it is in the form of a covenant: *I have made you mine, and you will always be mine.*

The book of Isaiah provides an example of this covenant. In a time of great difficulty and sorrow, the people of Israel said, "The LORD has forsaken me, my Lord has forgotten me." To this, God replied, "Can a woman forget her nursing child, or show no compassion for the child of her womb? Even these may forget, yet I will not forget you" (Isaiah 49:14-15).

The children's book *Mama, Do You Love Me?* reflects the covenant of baptism. Even though the child in the story causes some moments of pain and frustration, the mother says, "As long as the sun rises, I will love you."[2]

Ponder the depths of the covenant that God has made with you. Think of the deep love that God has for you, which is announced in baptism.

This is the same covenant that God wishes for and gives to people in your family, your work, and your community. It is the same covenant that God has made with the earth. It is the same covenant that God has established with all those who eat and drink with you at the table of the Lord.

PRAY

+ Spend time reflecting on this covenant of love.
+ Take out your life card and ask God to help you see the people and things listed there through the eyes of Christ.

O Love that will not let us go, we give you thanks for the covenant you make with us in baptism. The depth and surety of your love is hard for us to fathom. Help us to trust and to relax into that deep love. May our daily use of water be a reminder of your love for us. We pray in the name of Jesus. Amen.

DAY 45, WEDNESDAY

What Gifts or Benefits Does Baptism Grant?

It brings about forgiveness of sins,
redeems from death and the devil,
and gives eternal salvation to all who believe it,
as the words and promise of God declare. (SC)

PAUSE AND REFLECT

Earlier in this journey with the Small Catechism we looked at the forces of evil at work in the world and in your own life. We come to the waters of baptism seeking to renounce this evil:

> Do you renounce the devil and all the forces that defy God?
> **I renounce them.**
> Do you renounce the powers of this world that rebel against God?
> **I renounce them.**
> Do you renounce the ways of sin that draw you from God?
> **I renounce them.**[3]

Grace opens your eyes to see the power of evil that is within and around. The power of Christ at work in the waters of baptism delivers you from the captivity of sin and death. You need not fear death, for you have been incorporated into the death and the resurrection of Christ. You need not fear sin, for you stand forgiven and empowered for the new life of God to flow through you.

This deliverance is a journey. Along the journey you may be tempted to believe that your sin is not forgiven by Christ, that the power of evil is stronger than the power of God, or that death will capture and hold you in its grasp. Read the story of the woman at the well in John 4, or the story of Lazarus in John 11. In both stories the encounter with Jesus brings deliverance and newness of life. Old patterns are broken. New relationships are established. Jesus says of Lazarus, "Unbind him, and let him go" (John 11:44).

PRAY

+   Give thanks to God for the ways in which you already recognize that you are delivered from the power of sin and death.

+ Look at your life card and consider the ways in which sin and death are at work in the people who touch your life in the community in which you live and work. Ask God to show you how you can be a witness to the power of Christ to bring deliverance and new life.

God, our renewal and our strength, we confess that we continue to sin through our actions, our inactions, and even our thoughts. We give thanks for the forgiveness we find in you. Help us to continue to walk in your ways of new life and to renounce the evil that we find around and inside us. Give us eyes to clearly see evil, ears to hear it, minds keen to discern it, and a heart and will to confront it. We pray for those we know who are in the grip of evil. May they come to know your life-giving truth. We pray in your delivering name. Amen.

DAY 46, THURSDAY

[Baptism] brings about forgiveness of sins,
redeems from death and the devil,
and gives eternal salvation to all who believe it,
as the words and promise of God declare. (SC)

PAUSE AND REFLECT

Martin Luther describes the wonderful gift of God in baptism as salvation. Many people think of salvation as something that happens when you die and go to heaven, but it is not only something you wait for; it is something given to you now. Salvation means wholeness of body, mind, and spirit. It means wholeness for all people to live in a new relationship, and wholeness for the earth. The Old Testament word for this is *shalom*, which means "peace." Baptism puts you on the salvation road, the road to shalom. This is both gift and call.

Even as God is now at work in you, so God is at work in all the world to bring salvation. No power, no evil, no authority, no addiction, no illness, no sin, no catastrophe can destroy this promise given to you and to the whole world.

A person with the promise of salvation is a person of hope. Your hope rests in God, who is present with you and present in the world. Look at your life card and think of this promise of God as it relates to the different areas of your life.

How does the promise of salvation change your vision of the world?

PRAY

+ Consider how God is at work in you. Give thanks for what God is doing in your life.
+ Reflect on the relationships listed on your life card—with work, family, your church and community, and the environment. Give thanks for the ways God is at work in and through these relationships.

God of shalom, you promise us salvation, wholeness of life, not just in the future, but now. Help us to grasp and grow into your shalom and to work to bring it forth in the world around us. Strengthen us to live in your hope every day, no matter what life brings us. Enable us to share that hope with those around us. We pray in your peace and your hope. Amen.

DAY 47, FRIDAY

How Can Water Do Such Great Things?

Clearly the water does not do it,
but the word of God,
which is with and alongside the water,
and faith,
which trusts this word of God in the water. (SC)

PAUSE AND REFLECT

God is present in the water of baptism. This water of baptism is water of promise. Through this water connected to the promise, God becomes known. Through this promise of God, we come to see that God fills all creation and is present in all water.

Recall images of water that have brought you joy. Perhaps these include a warm bath or shower, refreshing rain, or a waterfall full of life and power. Think of the laughter, the joy, the surprise, the taste that accompanies water.

This water, so basic to life, is one of the elements God has chosen to reveal special promise. Does this not say that God is concerned about the basic elements of our lives?

Water, clean and pure, brings life. Water fills every pore of your body and every living thing. Lack of water brings death. Water polluted and misused also brings death. This basic substance is chosen by God as the sign of new life through baptism.

Water accompanied by the word of God brings new life to you. As in the story of creation, the Spirit hovers over the water and God speaks to create. Now in baptism the word and water are the vehicles God uses to create something in you. The water that you use and enjoy every day can remind you of your baptism.

God has put us in touch with the basic, daily element of water in our baptism. Can this be a call for us to hear and to respond to the basic call of water for all? The United Nations once set a goal of having fresh water within the reach of every person on the earth. We have not come close to achieving this goal. We have wells that have gone bad, streams of water that carry death, lakes and beaches with pollution warnings. For several years people in Flint, Michigan, were not able to drink the water due to lead contamination. In Canada many First Nations are under boil-water advisories and have been without fresh water for decades.

The apostle Paul talks about the whole creation "groaning in labor pains" and waiting to be delivered (Romans 8:22). Is God calling you to care for creation and for the water around you? What can you and your parish do to join with others in the life-giving work of caring for water?

PRAY

+ Remember that God is present in water. Spend time giving thanks throughout the day as you are in touch with water.

+ Look at your life card and ask God to help you see how baptism and the environment are tied together.

Creating God, you separated the water into oceans, lakes, rivers, and streams. You gave your people, the Israelites, water to drink in the desert. We give you thanks for this life-giving gift. Strengthen us to be good stewards of this gift in our communities, in our countries, and around the world. As we steward water, help us to also steward your word. Remind us that you call each of us, like Jesus, your beloved child in whom you are well pleased. In your life-giving name we pray. Amen.

DAY 48, SATURDAY

How Can Water Do Such Great Things?

Clearly the water does not do it,
but the word of God,
which is with and alongside the water,
and faith,
which trusts this word of God in the water. (SC)

PAUSE AND REFLECT

God has often used water as a vehicle to convey grace and salvation. Through water, Noah and his family were saved. Through the waters of the Nile River, the infant Moses was saved. Through the waters of the Sea of Reeds, the escaping children of Israel were saved. Through water from a rock, God provided relief for the thirsty Israelites in the desert. Through the waters of the Jordan River, the people of Israel went on to claim a new land and a new life. Through that same water of the Jordan, the leader Naaman was cleansed and healed of leprosy. Through the waters of the Jordan, John the Baptist called people to start life anew, and called Israel to once again shine the light of hope that comes from God. And through the waters of the Jordan, Jesus was baptized and then began his ministry.

In baptism God uses both water and the word to convey grace and salvation. Water and the word wash over you in baptism, and God's saving work is announced for you.

After Martin Luther was excommunicated from the church of his time, when he was tempted to despair, he wrote on the floor of his room, "I have been baptized." Despite the circumstances, he clung to the fact that he had been washed with water and God's word.

PRAY

+ Thank God for this water and this saving word of God. When you wash or shower or use water in any form today, give thanks that through word and water you have been brought into the reign of God. You know who you are—you are a child of God.

+ After baptism, Jesus began his ministry. How is God calling you to minister?

God, you continue to save your people through water and the word. Help us to be part of your saving work. Strengthen the work of baptism within us that we, like Luther, can rely on your covenant with us in the face of all adversity. Enable us to look on one another as your beloved children and treat one another with your love and grace. In your overflowing grace we pray. Amen.

DAY 49, SUNDAY

On this Sunday you are invited to join the community at worship and prayer. As you gather for worship, keep in mind that God calls people into service through the needs of the community. Is there some way you can use your gifts to help others and support the mission of the parish? Consider discussing this with others in your community.

PRAY

God of refreshment and renewal, be with us as we gather for worship this day. As we enter into worship, remind us of baptism and your saving action in our lives. May your grace rain down on all communities who gather in your name. Give to us all your living water, and transform our lives into worship and service of you. In Jesus' name we pray. Amen.

DAY 50, MONDAY

*I baptize you in the name of the Father, and of the
Son, and of the Holy Spirit.*[4]

PAUSE AND REFLECT

We know God more as a verb than as a noun. We know God through God's actions. In baptism God acts to claim us. In fact, God, the Father, and the Son, and the Holy Spirit, is revealed in action.

In baptism God brings you into a community or fellowship of people claimed by the action of God. Every time this community meets, your identity is announced. You meet in the name of the Father, and of the Son, and of the Holy Spirit. At worship you are greeted with the words "The grace of our Lord Jesus Christ, the love of God, and the communion of the Holy Spirit be with you all."[5]

The words used in your baptism will surround you in the church throughout your life. They mark your beginnings as well as your death. In the years in between, you will gather with other Christians in many places and circumstances, and be reminded of your baptism through these words. Each time you meet or gather in the name of God or make the sign of the cross, you are remembering your baptism.

In baptism you also become part of God's activity in the world. You are now a person incorporated into God in the name of the Father, Son, and Holy Spirit, and called to be part of God's creating, healing, and sanctifying action. Young and old and midlife folk—regardless of gender, sexuality, ethnicity, background, income, health, abilities—all are swept up in baptism into God's action and called to be a part of God's work.

You have been given the gift of knowing that in baptism God claims you, brings you into community with others who are baptized, and calls you to be part of God's work in the world.

PRAY

+ Consider that instead of praying to God, the Father, and the Son, and the Holy Spirit, some people use other formulations like Creator, Redeemer, and Sanctifier. What do you think? How do you address the triune God?

- Remember people who are in your parish. Pray for them and their part in the action of God.
- Take out your life card and think of yourself as one who is a part of the action of God in all of the areas of your life. Ask God to help you to prioritize ways to take part in God's action.

Holy Trinity, love divine, we thank and praise you for the gift of baptism. You have claimed us as your own. We are honoured that through baptism you envelop us into your action and call us to be part of your work. We celebrate that we are also joined with others through baptism, those both like and unlike ourselves. Help us to welcome and work with all the baptized, delighting that we are all part of your reign of grace. In the name of your threefold being we pray. Amen.

DAY 51, TUESDAY

[God] saved us . . . according to [God's] mercy, through the water of rebirth and renewal by the Holy Spirit.

Titus 3:5

PAUSE AND REFLECT

In his Small Catechism, Martin Luther uses this scripture text from Titus to help people understand the gift of baptism as a washing of rebirth.

The church did not always emphasize washing as a part of baptism. For a time, a small amount of water was used, and no washing seemed to take place in baptism. Today we seek to call attention to this aspect of baptism, using bigger baptismal fonts and larger amounts of water. Immersion is used in some situations, and fonts often contain enough water to represent washing.

Something is washed away in baptism. In the early church, as a person came forward for baptism, their clothes were stripped off as a sign of leaving their former life and taking on the life of Christ. The floodwaters of baptism wash away all of those things that hinder life in its fullness—greed, anger, exploitation, carelessness, manipulation of others, selfish hoarding of goods, unwillingness to share with others, indifference to others and creation.

We know that some habits die hard, and temptations poke up their heads every day, attempting to drag us back into old, selfish ways of thinking. Luther writes that the washing of rebirth continues each day as "all sins and evil desires [are] drowned and die through daily sorrow for sin and through repentance" (SC). This process unfolds before us by the grace of God. It is a lifelong journey.

PRAY

+ Consider those things that tempt you to return to an old way of thinking and living. Remember that in the midst of this you are claimed by the God who will use you for God's work.

+ Some habits and behaviors are so pernicious that you may need help from others. Do not hesitate to talk about issues like these with your pastor.

+ Give thanks to God, for God has the power to change all things and make them new.

Washerwoman God, in baptism you wash away our sins. In our daily repentance and remembrance of baptism you continue to wash away our sins. Strengthen in us the will to drown all selfish desires. Help us to resist temptation. Take away the clothing of our old lives, and clothe us in the righteous garments of Christ. In your cleansing and renewing name we pray. Amen.

DAY 52, WEDNESDAY

*... through the water of rebirth and
renewal by the Holy Spirit.*

Titus 3:5

*Daily a new person is to come forth
and rise up to live before God
in righteousness and purity forever.* (SC)

PAUSE AND REFLECT

A man named Lazarus dies and is placed in a tomb. Jesus gets to the tomb three days later and shouts, "Lazarus, come out!" Lazarus does come forth, enveloped by grave clothes. Jesus says, "Unbind him, and let him go" (John 11:44).

This is our baptismal story, for this is what happens in baptism. New life springs forth. Old ways of bondage are torn away so that we might live in freedom and new life in God. The apostle Paul explains the things that bind us in these terms: "fornication, impurity, licentiousness, idolatry, sorcery, enmities, strife, jealousy, anger, quarrels, dissensions, factions, envy, drunkenness, carousing, and things like these" (Galatians 5:19-21).

"Unbind him, and let him go," Jesus says of Lazarus. Let the new life come forth. Let something new be generated in the hearts of human beings. Paul says this newness will be characterized by "love, joy, peace, patience, kindness, generosity, faithfulness, gentleness, and self-control" (Galatians 5:22-23).

This newness is a part of God's new creation in you.

PRAY

+ Look at the different areas on your life card. Where do you see God at work in and around you? Where is God calling you to be at work?

+ Pray for help in recognizing the old in your life that still needs to go, as well as the new that the Spirit is calling out.

+ Pray for the church and the world, that the Spirit of God will cause something new and life-giving to spring forth.

God of new life, every day you call us to leave the ways of bondage and live in the freedom of life in you. Continue to create new hearts within us. Liberate us to work to free others who are in bondage. We pray in the name of your freedom and grace. Amen.

DAY 53, THURSDAY

We give you thanks, O God, that through water and the Holy Spirit you give your daughters and sons new birth, cleanse them from sin, and raise them to eternal life. Sustain [name] with the gift of your Holy Spirit: the spirit of wisdom and understanding, the spirit of counsel and might, the spirit of knowledge and the fear of the Lord, the spirit of joy in your presence, both now and forever.[6]

PAUSE AND REFLECT

Sometimes other Christians will ask you if you have received the Holy Spirit. The Spirit has been present throughout your journey of life. The Spirit was present to breathe life into you at birth. The Spirit was present to call you into the life of the church. The Spirit was present in the washing and in the laying on of hands. Have you received the Holy Spirit? Absolutely!

This hymn recalls what happens to the baptized:

This is the Spirit's entry now:
the water and the Word,
the cross of Jesus on your brow,
the seal both felt and heard.

This miracle of life reborn
comes from the Lord of breath;
the sinless one from life was torn;
our life comes through his death.

Let water be the sacred sign
that we must die each day
to rise again by his design
as foll'wers of his way.

Renewing Spirit, hear our praise
for your baptismal pow'r
that washes us through all our days.
Come, cleanse again this hour.[7]

The Spirit of God stirs in you. The power of God, present in creation, is present in you, a new creation. God's intent and hope are that this new creation will grow and flourish and bring joy to those who are a part of your life.

PRAY

+ Spend some time in the presence of God, giving thanks for the Spirit and the new life that lives in you. You are born again, a new creature in God's world.

+ Pray for the renewing Spirit's work within and through your parish.

Renewing Spirit, hear our praise. Continue to renew us so that we are born again in you. Thank you for your presence with us in birth, throughout our lives, in death, and in the new life we are promised. Open our eyes and our hearts to see your presence in our lives and in the lives of others. We pray in the name of the Lord of breath. Amen.

DAY 54, FRIDAY

[Name], child of God, you have been sealed by the Holy Spirit and marked with the cross of Christ forever.[8]

PAUSE AND REFLECT

In a service of welcoming baptismal candidates to the catechumenate, candidates have the sign of the cross marked on them as the people say the following prayers.

Receive the cross on your forehead, a sign of God's endless love and mercy for you. Learn to know Christ and to follow him.
Glory and praise to you, almighty God.

Receive the cross on your ears, that you may hear the Gospel of Christ, the word of life.
Glory and praise to you, almighty God.

Receive the cross on your eyes, that you may see the light of Christ, illumination for your way.
Glory and praise to you, almighty God.

Receive the cross on your lips, that you may sing the praise of Christ, the joy of the church.
Glory and praise to you, almighty God.

Receive the cross on your heart, that God may dwell there by faith.
Glory and praise to you, almighty God.

Receive the cross on your shoulders, that you may bear the gentle yoke of Christ.
Glory and praise to you, almighty God.

Receive the cross on your hands, that God's mercy may be known in your work.
Glory and praise to you, almighty God.

Receive the cross on your feet, that you may walk in the way of Christ.
Glory and praise to you, almighty God.[9]

The call of baptism is a call to a life lived under the cross. It is a call to use all of the gifts God has given you in the service of God and others.

PRAY

+ As you pray, make the sign of the cross and remember God's gifts and call to you in baptism.

- ✦ Give thanks that you are a part of God's new creation.

- ✦ Consider the gifts God has given you. Look at your life card. In what areas are there possibilities for using your gifts? How will you place these gifts in the service of God? Ask God to help you.

God of new creation, in baptism you mark us with the sign of the cross and seal us with your Spirit. Help us to remember that you have claimed us and called us to take up our crosses and follow in your way of life and truth. Give us strength to use the gifts you have given us in service of you. We pray under the sign of the cross. Amen.

DAY 55, SATURDAY

Daily a new person is to come forth
and rise up to live before God . . . (SC)

PAUSE AND REFLECT

Daily a new person is to come forth and rise up. This is not to be like the main character in the movie *Groundhog Day* (Columbia Pictures, 1993), who continually repeats the same day. In baptism, in the Spirit's daily renewal, refreshment, and forgiveness, each day is a new and different day, and we have the chance to live new and forgiven lives—not forgetting yesterday or all our yesterdays, but with the chance to start afresh.

We can start afresh in our close relationships and be more loving and caring companions. We can start again in our relationship with the earth and take greater care of creation. We can start aright in our relationship with God and walk more closely in following Jesus. We can start anew in our work and be more diligent and more balanced in our lives. We can start afresh in our relationship with community and take more responsibility, or move aside and let others share in leadership.

How is the Spirit moving in your life? Look at the hymn "Spirit of Gentleness" (ELW 396), if possible. Is the Spirit being gentle in your life right now? Is it restless? Is it stirring you from placidness?

PRAY

+ Ask God to help you see the work of the Spirit in and around you.

+ Take out your life card and consider the areas in your life where the Spirit may be moving today. Pray for the work of the Spirit in your family, work, parish, and community, and in the environment.

Spirit of gentleness, call us to rise up to live before God. Spirit of restlessness, stir us out of complacency to more freely love and share and work for freedom everywhere. Open our ears and hearts to hear your call. Awaken us to feel your stirrings within. Give us the courage to say yes to your invitation to follow. In your gentle and restless name we pray. Amen.

DAY 56, SUNDAY

Today is Sunday. Christians meet on the first day of the week to celebrate Jesus' resurrection. We call this the eighth day of creation. The new creation comes into being through the work of Christ. You are a part of that new creation.

Return to the baptismal font this morning and recall your baptism. (Your font may have eight sides to represent the eighth day of creation.) Give thanks for the new life that flows through you. Ask God to show you how this new life can be manifest in your world.

PRAY

God of new creation, as we gather in worship, we remember our baptism and give thanks for the new life that flows in us. Help us to look at our siblings in Christ and see the new life flowing in them. Strengthen us in living our baptismal covenant with you and with one another. Open our minds and hearts to the new things to which you call us as individuals, as communities, and as the whole church. In your creating name we pray. Amen.

DAY 57, MONDAY

Clothed with Christ in baptism, the newly baptized may receive a baptismal garment.[10]

PAUSE AND REFLECT

Martin Luther said that we stand before the cross as beggars with the torn and tattered clothes of our lives, but Christ comes and covers us with new robes of righteousness that will last throughout our days.

These robes call us to live in the justice and peace of God. They prepare us for the great banquet when Christ will draw all things to God. These robes are not to be stored away for some future feast, but to be worn knowing that the feast of Christ's rule has already begun.

In the early church, a newly baptized person was to wear a white robe throughout the season of Easter. Today many ministers in the church, both lay and clergy, wear robes or albs during worship as a reminder of the robes of baptism.

In baptism God covers us with Christ's righteousness, calls us to live in justice and peace, and prepares us for the feast of Christ's reign. We are signs in the world of this reign of God. We point to the rule of Christ through what we do and what we wear:

> As God's chosen ones, holy and beloved, clothe yourselves with compassion, kindness, humility, meekness, and patience. Bear with one another and, if anyone has a complaint against another, forgive each other; just as the Lord has forgiven you, so you also must forgive. Above all, clothe yourselves with love, which binds everything together in perfect harmony (Colossians 3:12-14).

This is the garment God calls us to wear each day.

PRAY

- Take out your life card and consider the feast already present in your family, work, community, and environment. Where do you feel called by God as one who wears the righteousness of God?

- Pray that God will enlighten you to see glimpses of the reign of Christ in your life today. What might you do to point to this reign of Christ?

+ Pray for your parish, your synod, and the church, that they would point to the gentle rule of Christ, the Lamb of God.

Mothering God, you clothe us in robes of righteousness—Christ's righteousness—garments made too big so that we can grow into them. We pray that we would look at others; see on them the same made-right-with-God attire; and honour, respect, and love them for your sake. Thank you for your ongoing, loving, and tender care of us. In your bountiful name we pray. Amen.

DAY 58, TUESDAY

Let your light shine before others, so that they may see
your good works and give glory to your Father in heaven.

Matthew 5:16

PAUSE AND REFLECT

The light from the Easter Vigil or paschal candle is given to you at baptism as a sign of your call to be a light in the world. The words above from the Gospel of Matthew accompany the gift of a lighted candle to the newly baptized.

Again take out your life card and consider your world. Consider your family, your work, your community, and the environment. It is to this world that Christ sends you to bear light.

The Matthew 5 text suggests that it will be through your works in the world that God will be glorified. You carry the light of Christ in you, and it shows in what you do. What you say may be important, but here the emphasis is on giving glory to God through what you do.

Spend time considering what you will do in your family, your work, your community, and the environment in the next twenty-four hours. Think of the people you will meet, the strangers you may greet, and the work that you will do. Imagine that, as you come into contact with people, this will give glory to God.

You will not be able to imagine everything that will take place. You will have your schedule interrupted by people and unknown events. Ask God to help you to handle these interruptions. Ask God to let the light of Christ shine forth in you this day. Remember that in Christ the distinction between sacred and secular has broken down. All is holy, for all is under the saving plan of God. Everything you do is sacred.

Now, do not get uptight and start to think that everything has to be done in a perfect way. God gives you freedom to respond in ways that are unique to you. Set aside these twenty-four hours as belonging to God. At the end of this period, recall what has happened and then give thanks to God for the grace you experienced during this time.

PRAY

+ Give thanks for the light of Christ and ask God to help you let it shine.

+ Take out your life card and consider the ways in which the light of Christ could shine in all areas of your life.

Light of the world, we give you thanks and praise for the new life and light you give to us in baptism. Strengthen within us the desire to shine your light through our actions. Like lighthouse keepers, may we keep this light shining in our world to give glory and honour to you. In your bright and glorious name we pray. Amen.

DAY 59, WEDNESDAY

Let us welcome the newly baptized.
**We welcome you into the body of Christ and
into the mission we share:
join us in giving thanks and praise to God
and bearing God's creative and redeeming word
to all the world.**[11]

PAUSE AND REFLECT

Martin Luther would be pleased to know that the baptismal service we use today emphasizes a concept important to him. You are a member of the priesthood we all share in Christ Jesus.

In spite of the strong emphasis Luther and the Reformation placed on the concept of the priesthood of believers, it is not easy for us to think of ourselves as part of a priesthood. We tend to think that this relates to the clergy and not to laity. But while the concept has often been neglected in the church, it is still vital: All of the baptized are the people of God and belong to the priesthood of all believers. Through baptism each believer shares in the work of Christ.

You may be a person who deals mostly with the creative ministry of Christ. You may be an engineer, a farmer, a builder, a garbage collector; you may work with computers or new technologies. You may be a fisher, a logger, or a shoemaker; you may work in the auto industry. Your part in the ministry of Christ is creativity or building.

On the other hand, you may be a doctor, a lawyer, a nurse, or a counselor. You may be a parent raising a child. You are caring for people and seeking to heal the world. Your work is dealing with redemption.

These two parts of the body of Christ, creative and redeeming, need to work together. They are both part of the work of Christ. While the church has given much time and thought to the area of healing and redemption, it has often neglected the work of creativity. Perhaps you can help lead the church in the creative ministry of Christ.

You as creator or as healer are part of the priesthood of the body of Christ. Your work is to be offered up for the sake of the world. For this you have been baptized and called.

PRAY

+ In your meditation today, ask God to help you discover how you are a part of the mission of Christ. Are you a creator or a healer? You may be involved in both aspects of ministry, but perhaps thinking about this distinction will help you to hear the call of Christ.

+ Pray for all those who are healers—for pastors, doctors, physiotherapists, counselors, social workers, and others who are a part of the redeeming work of Christ.

+ Pray for all those who are creators—those who feed, clothe, house, and transport people, and make the world beautiful.

Christ our High Priest, we thank you for calling us all to serve in your priesthood. Strengthen the gifts of ministry you have given us, that we may be creators and healers with you. Help us to honour the work that each of us does in your priesthood. Give us insight to see that categories of lay and clergy are not hierarchical, but rather different ways we are called to serve as your priestly people. In your holy name we pray. Amen.

DAY 60, THURSDAY

The peace of God, which surpasses all understanding,
will guard your hearts and your minds in Christ Jesus.

Philippians 4:7

PAUSE AND REFLECT

As baptized children of God we are called to follow Christ's way of peace—to be people of peace and to work for peace wherever we find ourselves.

In the Hebrew Scriptures, the word for peace is *shalom*, which means peace with God, peace with other people, and peace with the land. Shalom is the hope for all people and all the world. This hope for shalom is now your hope.

Ask God to make you a worker for peace—peace in your family, peace in your work, peace in your neighbourhood, peace with the land. Consider what this means for you.

PRAY

+ Let this prayer attributed to Francis of Assisi be the basis of your meditation and prayer for today.

> Lord, make us instruments of your peace. Where there is hatred, let us sow love; where there is injury, pardon; where there is discord, union; where there is doubt, faith; where there is despair, hope; where there is darkness, light; where there is sadness, joy. Grant that we may not so much seek to be consoled as to console; to be understood as to understand; to be loved as to love. For it is in giving that we receive; it is in pardoning that we are pardoned; and it is in dying that we are born to eternal life. Amen.[12]

Christ our peace, we pray that we may embody your spirit of shalom. We confess to you the lack of peace in our world, in our communities, and even in our homes. Help us to bring about peace with one another and indeed with all creation. Strengthen us in our baptismal covenant so that we may daily follow your way of peace and justice. In your peaceful and just name we pray. Amen.

DAY 61, FRIDAY

Therefore we have been buried with him by baptism into death, so that, just as Christ was raised from the dead by the glory of the Father, so we too might walk in newness of life.

Romans 6:4

PAUSE AND REFLECT

Spend today's time of prayer and reflection in silence, asking to be shown God's grace in your life.

PRAY

+ Recall the past several days of prayer and reflection on baptism. What has become important to you? What do you see as your mission in the church? Perhaps you have already found ways to respond to God's grace in your life. Perhaps God is calling you to new ways and new people.

+ Look at your life card. Perhaps there are things or people you would like to add. Do you see the areas of your life differently, now that you have begun to look at them through the eyes of your baptism?

+ Offer thanks to God for the gifts that God has given in your life over the past few days.

God, we thank you for continuing to strengthen us in faith and renew your baptismal covenant with us. Thank you for the gift of these days of reflection. Help us to continue to cling to the promises you make to us in baptism. Strengthen us to live out the promises we make in baptism. We pray in your covenantal love. Amen.

GIFTS OF GOD

DAY 62, SATURDAY

For as in one body we have many members, and not all the members have the same function, so we, who are many, are one body in Christ, and individually we are members one of another. We have gifts that differ according to the grace given to us: prophecy, in proportion to faith; ministry, in ministering; the teacher, in teaching; the exhorter, in exhortation; the giver, in generosity; the leader, in diligence; the compassionate, in cheerfulness.

Romans 12:4-8

PAUSE AND REFLECT

The apostle Paul's list in Romans 12:4-8 is not exhaustive, but only hints at the many gifts that God gives us.

What gifts has God given to you? This may be a difficult question for you to answer right now. Identifying your gifts requires some thought and prayer, as well as the honest assessment of trusted friends and community members.

PRAY

+ Spend time today asking God to help you to recognize the gifts given to you by the Spirit.
+ Consider who might help you to identify what your gifts are and how you might use them in Christ's ministry.
+ Give thanks for the gifts God has given you. Pray that you might appreciate them.
+ Some gifts will become evident at different times in your life. Pray that God would show you gifts that have not yet been revealed to you.
+ Take out your life card and think of your gifts in relationship to the areas of your life.

Giver of gifts, we thank you for all the gifts you shower on your creation. Give us discernment to discover our gifts and to help others discover and develop their gifts. Help us as individuals and a community to honour the gifts of others without comparisons or jealousy. Remind us that the gifts you give us are meant for sharing with all of God's beloved. In your generous name we pray. Amen.

DAY 63, SUNDAY

Sunday, the eighth day of creation, is a good time to join your siblings in Christ for community worship and prayer. After all, they are all part of God's new creation. As you participate in worship, think of the members of the community whom you know well. What gifts do they bring to the parish? Some examples are attending worship faithfully, sharing money generously, feeding the hungry, volunteering with programs that provide safe shelter, teaching, serving on a church committee, and assisting in worship. Thank God for the many ways people share their gifts in this community.

PRAY

We praise and bless you, O God, for you call us into community. We thank you for the gifts you have given us in one another. As we worship today, help us to notice and to appreciate the gifts of those around us and the ways these gifts are used to your glory. Empower us to continue to bring forth your gifts in one another. In your lavish and generous name we pray. Amen.

DAY 64, MONDAY

*The fruit of the Spirit is love, joy, peace,
patience, kindness, generosity, faithfulness,
gentleness, and self-control.*

Galatians 5:22-23

PAUSE AND REFLECT

Love, joy, peace, patience, kindness, generosity, faithfulness, gentleness, and self-control. Which of these gifts is yours? Read the list again and find one gift that best suits you or who you would like to be.

You might say, "I wish I were more patient" or "I have one gift, but I am missing a lot of the others." But instead of focusing on what you do not have, celebrate and thank God for the gift you have.

Imagine being in a community in which each person brings just one gift. Others would bring gifts that you may be lacking. Together this would be a strong community.

In the community of Christ, we are strong together. We recognize, celebrate, and give thanks for everyone's gifts. Our gifts are not just for our personal use and benefit, but for the body of Christ. And in turn, the body of Christ serves the world.

What gifts do you bring to the body of Christ? What gifts do others bring?

PRAY

+ Take time to look at the centre of your life card. There is your name, and you are under the cross. Give thanks for the gifts that the Spirit has given to you.

+ Spend time giving thanks for the gifts you see in others. How will you tell people about the gifts you see in them?

Giver of all gifts, in you all gifts are present. We confess that we sometimes hoard our gifts. Help us to know and honour the gifts that we have been given, and to share them freely. Strengthen within us the ability and desire to lift up the gifts of others. Remind us that our gifts work best when joined with the gifts of others for the benefit of all creation. We pray with hearts full of thankfulness. Amen.

DAY 65, TUESDAY

O LORD, you have searched me and known me.
You know when I sit down and when I rise up;
*   you discern my thoughts from far away.*
You search out my path and my lying down,
*   and are acquainted with all my ways.*
Even before a word is on my tongue,
*   O LORD, you know it completely. . . .*

For it was you who formed my inward parts;
*   you knit me together in my mother's womb.*
I praise you, for I am fearfully and wonderfully made.
*   Wonderful are your works;*
that I know very well.

Psalm 139:1-4, 13-14

PAUSE AND REFLECT

You are a gift from God. God has placed you on the earth and given you all that makes you a person. Wonderful are God's works!

Much in life contradicts this pronouncement God makes about you. Our society too often says that you are wonderful *if* you are rich, young, thin, physically energetic, happy, and so on. These unrealistic standards result in many of us feeling that we have little value because we do not "measure up."

An older woman who uses a wheelchair was persuaded to attend a church retreat. The retreat participants considered their God-given gifts and how they might use these gifts for Christ's ministry. The woman thought that she had little to give in comparison to other people. She left the retreat very discouraged.

Days later she called the pastor with a new spirit in her voice. She volunteered to call and greet members, on behalf of the parish, on their birthdays, anniversaries, and other important days in their lives. She is now well acquainted with most members of the parish, and calls several regularly to share in their joys and their burdens. She recognized that she has a gift for reaching out to others, and now uses it to serve Christ and the world.

PRAY

+ Thank God that you are wonderfully made.

+ Ask God to help you discover your gifts and the means to share them with others and participate in the ministry of Christ.

Creating God, in you we are fearfully and wonderfully made. Teach us to appreciate the wonder in ourselves and in one another. Empower us to work to end bullying that demeans the wonder of your creation in individuals. Support us in holding out against the pressures of our culture to be perfect. Strengthen our ability to talk about these things and to support one another. In your wonder-full name we pray. Amen.

DAY 66, WEDNESDAY

Like clouds and wind without rain
is one who boasts of a gift never given.

Proverbs 25:14

PAUSE AND REFLECT

Tomorrow we will turn to Luther's explanation of holy communion in the Small Catechism. For today, ask for God's guidance as you look again at your call to serve Christ and others.

Take out your life card and think of things that you might do in the four areas of your life. When you consider the gifts that God has given you, and the places in which you now find yourself in your family, community, work, and environment, what stands out to you? Which things do you feel strongly called to do? Consider any talents and skills that you may need to develop to do these things well, and the time it might take to prepare yourself for such work. Are there things that you will have to give up, obstacles to overcome, or risks you may have to take to do this?

Perhaps it is difficult for you to consider that you have gifts from the Spirit and that God has placed you on the earth to serve Christ and others with these gifts. Take time to seek help from God and from members of your church community.

God loves you and gives you much freedom in finding ways to use your gifts—ways that suit you well and bring joy to others and all creation.

PRAY

+ Give thanks to God for the freedom to try different ways of using your gifts.
+ Give thanks to God for the gifts that you already recognize in yourself, and ask God to reveal other gifts to you.
+ Pray for God's guidance in helping others to recognize and actualize their gifts in their lives.

God, you know us better than we know ourselves. Open our eyes and ears to the ways you are calling us to use our gifts in our families, communities, work, and creation. If we are not hearing you, give us courage to ask others for help in listening and discerning. We thank you for the freedom to try things and make mistakes, knowing that nothing will take away your love. In your loving name we pray. Amen.

HOLY COMMUNION

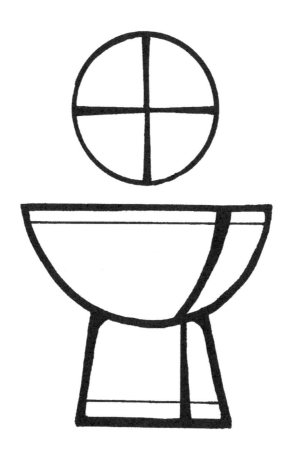

DAY 67, THURSDAY

The peace of Christ be with you always.
And also with you.[1]

PAUSE AND REFLECT

We will turn to the "Sacrament of the Altar" portion of the Small Catechism for the next couple of weeks. This sacrament has many names: eucharist (from a Greek word meaning "thanksgiving"), holy communion, the Lord's supper, the last supper, the table of the Lord. Each name calls attention to a different emphasis on the meal.

In Sunday worship the sharing of the peace marks a transition between the Service of the Word and the eucharist. You and other worshipers are invited to greet one another with the peace of the Lord. Through this gesture you affirm the presence of Christ among us. The peace that you share is a sign of reconciliation between people in the community. Hurts are forgiven, sins are pardoned, quarrels are encouraged to come to an end. All worshipers are a part of the reconciling body of Christ.

On Thursday, Day 60, the Hebrew concept of peace or shalom was described as peace between God, the people, and the environment. It was for this peace that Israel prayed. When we share the peace of Christ in worship, we are calling for this shalom to be present in our lives, in the lives of others, and in the world. Shalom means hospitality and welcoming the stranger in our midst, and even more, the yearning of the church for reconciliation in the whole world.

As Christians we share this greeting of peace before celebrating the eucharist. After the worship service we go forth as agents of reconciliation, carrying the peace of Christ with us.

PRAY

+ Take out your life card and consider the need for peace in each area of your life.
+ Ask God to lead you as an agent of reconciliation. Pray for wisdom and courage to be one who brings peace into the world.

Reconciling Christ, yours is the way of peace and forgiveness. Give us hearts and minds to fully understand that, in sharing your peace with others, we are laying down our hurts and resentments. Even more so, remind us that once we lay these things down, we are not to pick them up again. Strengthen within us the will to do the hard work of reconciliation in all areas of our lives. Empower us to go into the world as agents of your reconciling power. With hearts full of your shalom we pray. Amen.

DAY 68, FRIDAY

What Is the Sacrament of the Altar?

It is the true body and blood
of our Lord Jesus Christ
under the bread and wine,
instituted by Christ himself
for us Christians to eat and to drink.

WHERE IS THIS WRITTEN?

The holy evangelists, Matthew, Mark, and Luke, and
St. Paul write thus:

In the night in which he was betrayed,
our Lord Jesus took bread, and gave thanks;
broke it, and gave it to his disciples,
saying: Take and eat;
this is my body, given for you.
Do this for the remembrance of me.
Again, after supper, he took the cup,
gave thanks, and gave it for all to drink,
saying: This cup is the new covenant in my blood,
shed for you and for all people
for the forgiveness of sin.
Do this for the remembrance of me. (SC)

PAUSE AND REFLECT

During the Jewish festival of Passover, the followers of Jesus met to keep that sacred meal. The Passover meal was a feast of victory, as Jewish believers recalled with food, story, laughter, and dance how God freed the Israelites from slavery in Egypt. Liberated from slavery, the Israelites began the journey to a new land of hope.

In New Testament times the Romans held the Jews in bondage, so Jewish believers gathered in their homes to keep the Passover celebration and remember the liberation of God.

162

This is the meal that Jesus and his followers were sharing on the night when he was betrayed. That night's celebration must have been dulled by the threats that hung over Jesus and his followers. Yet despite the threats, there was the promise of victory.

PRAY

+ Spend time imagining that you are present with the other followers of Jesus. The whole company of Jesus, all genders, all abilities, all ages, all races, are in the upper room, and you are a part of them. What emotions do you feel? What is it like to have a celebration with threats hanging over your head?

+ What emotions would you experience as Jesus takes both bread and wine from the table and says, "This is my body, given for you . . . this is the new covenant in my blood, shed for you and for all people . . . do this for the remembrance of me"?

+ Imagine that you take the bread and drink from the cup. How do you feel?

+ Close this time of meditation by thanking God for this experience.

Jesus, our hearts are full of many emotions as we meditate on joining you as a follower at the last supper. We give you thanks for the gifts of bread and wine, the gifts of your body and blood. Strengthen us through our participation in this holy meal. We turn to you with hearts full of love, and we worship you. In your precious name we pray. Amen.

DAY 69, SATURDAY

In the night in which he was betrayed,
our Lord Jesus took bread, and gave thanks;
broke it, and gave it to his disciples,
saying: Take and eat;
this is my body, given for you.
Do this for the remembrance of me. (SC)

PAUSE AND REFLECT

Today imagine that you are present in a home in Jerusalem after Pentecost. Jesus has been raised from the dead. Around a meal the followers of Jesus share bread and wine. They are under threat because the authorities want to stop them from talking about Jesus. Still, they gather for prayer and for this meal. You are one of them.

What emotions are you feeling?

When you take the bread and drink from the cup, what is going on inside you?

Does this remain a feast dulled by threat, or is this now a feast of victory?

PRAY

+ Thank God that through Christ you are a member of this company, the followers of Jesus.
+ Pray for the members of the parish who gather with you at Christ's table. Ask God to bless them and unite all of you in the body of Christ.

Christ of the fearful and the fearless, you continue to gather us at your table. Help us to recognize that, just as we approach this holy meal with emotions and needs that change week by week, so do others at the same table. Guide our prayers for one another as we come to the table, for concerns that we know, and for the concerns that we do not know. In your strengthening and comforting name we pray. Amen.

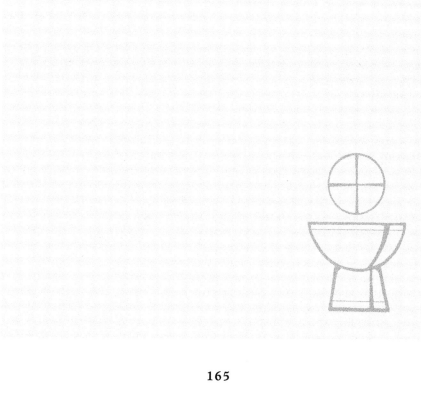

DAY 70, SUNDAY

Prepare yourself for today's community gathering in worship. Pray for the pastor and for the people as you meet around word and sacrament. Ask the Lord to continue to guide you as you search for ways to serve this community, and to make you aware of the needs of individuals and the church. Through this time of worship, God will help you to respond to others. Be aware too of the people serving within your community, and give thanks for them.

PRAY

Gathering God, we thank you that you bring us together as your body in many forms of worship all around the world. Whether we gather in person or online, in house churches, church buildings, outdoors, or in coffee shops, you promise to be with us when we gather. We give you thanks for the continued grace we receive through your sacraments. May our participation in your sacraments strengthen us to follow you in our daily living. Held together in your strong arms we pray. Amen.

DAY 71, MONDAY

Blessed are you, O God, maker of all things. Through your goodness you have blessed us with these gifts: our selves, our time, and our possessions. Use us, and what we have gathered, in feeding the world with your love, through the one who gave himself for us, Jesus Christ, our Savior and Lord.[2]

PAUSE AND REFLECT

Gifts of money, bread, and wine may be brought forward in the worship service. Then a pastor or worship assistant leads the congregation in the prayer above.

Take out your life card and consider all of the areas of your life. There is your name—and you are gift. There is your family—and this is gift. There is your work—and this is gift. There is your community—and this is gift. There is your environment—and this is gift. All of this you offer up along with the gifts of money, bread, and wine. It is not you alone who does this. You are joined in this offering by members of the congregation, and by Christians around the world, that all might be recreated in the likeness of Christ for use in the reign of God.

Pray this litany of thanksgiving today and offer all of yourself to God:

For the beauty and wonder of creation,
We thank you, Lord.

For all that is gracious in the lives of [people], revealing the image of Christ,
We thank you, Lord.

For our daily food, for our homes and families and friends,
We thank you, Lord.

For minds to think and hearts to love,
We thank you, Lord.

For health and strength, and skill to work, and for leisure to rest and play,
We thank you, Lord.

For those who are brave and courageous, patient in suffering and faithful in adversity,
We thank you, Lord.

For all those who pursue peace, justice, and truth,
We thank you, Lord.

For [names] and all the saints whose lives have reflected the light of Christ,
We thank you, Lord.[3]

PRAY

+ Spend time remembering all the gifts God has given you, and give thanks for them.

+ Give thanks for the gifts of the people in your family and of those with whom you work.

Maker of all things, we give you thanks for what we have. We confess that sometimes we are jealous of people who have more things. Remind us that there are many people who have less than we do. Help us to be generous with all that we have, to offer it back to you for the benefit of all your beloved people and all creation. We pray in your gifting name. Amen.

DAY 72, TUESDAY

Even as bread and wine become the body and blood of Christ, so the people are transformed into the body of Christ.[4]

PAUSE AND REFLECT

The eucharist is a meal of transformation.

In the reign of God the curse of human labour (see Genesis chapter 3) is transformed into a blessing. One can imagine, for example, all that goes into making a loaf of bread—cultivating, sowing, harvesting, gathering, grinding, mixing, kneading, baking, transporting, selling—in order to place this bread on the table. All this is given so that seed might be transformed into bread.

Bread and wine become the body and blood of Christ. We speak of a mystery here. The words of Jesus affirm his presence in the bread and wine. As in baptism, Jesus testifies that God is not hostile to creation, to the stuff of the earth. Simple gifts of bread and wine are transformed.

Along with bread and wine, we offer ourselves at the table, that we might be transformed, for we are a holy nation, a priesthood, an extraordinary group of people who are sent to care for others and the world. Luther writes:

> When you have partaken of this sacrament, therefore, or desire to partake of it, you must in turn share the misfortunes of the fellowship . . . all the unjust suffering of the innocent, with which the world is everywhere filled to overflowing. You must fight, work, pray and—if you cannot do more—have heartfelt sympathy.[5]

The world may see only the bread and the wine, but you see what God does at the table and are reminded that God's work of transformation continues around the world.

PRAY

+ Pray for insight to see signs of God's work of transformation taking place in your life and in the lives of others. Spend time thanking God for these signs.

+ Take out your life card and think about the people in your life. Do you see signs of God's transforming work in their lives? Ask God to guide you in supporting people in their faith during times of transformation.

+ Pray for transformation in the lives of all who are suffering. How might you be a part of this transforming work in your community or in the world?

God of transformation, around the world and in our own communities we see much suffering—poverty, addiction, human trafficking, disease, forced displacement due to war or climate change, racism, colonialism, oppression of many kinds—the list goes on and on. May your holy meal transform us so that we advocate, work, and pray to end the suffering of the innocents, who are also your beloved children. We pray in your just and holy name. Amen.

DAY 73, WEDNESDAY

Do this for the remembrance of me. (SC)

PAUSE AND REFLECT

Israel remembered the deliverance from Egypt during the yearly Passover celebration. To remember was to actually go through the experience again, thus each year the whole community participated in this deliverance.

When Jesus invites us to remember him, he invites us to journey with him through the cross and resurrection. In the eucharist we are invited to pass through this mystery and to be sustained by it. We are invited to follow Christ, take up the cross, and lay down our lives for the sake of others. Where will this lead us?

To remember Jesus is to follow him and his ministry. Jesus often found himself with people who were excluded: those who were poor, oppressed, and marginalized by society. Matthew 25 sees the Christ embracing people who are hungry, thirsty, naked, imprisoned, sick, and strangers. We are called to participate in this ministry of Jesus.

Listen to the words of Jürgen Moltmann:

> Anyone who celebrates the Lord's Supper in a world of hunger and oppression does so in complete solidarity with the hopes and sufferings of all . . . because . . . the Messiah invites all . . . to his table. . . . In the mysteries, the feast separates the initiated from the rest of the world. But Christ's messianic feast makes its participants one with the physically and spiritually hungry all over the world.[6]

Who are the ones excluded today? Who are the "physically and spiritually hungry"?

PRAY

+ Remember and pray for all who suffer in our world.
+ Remember all who are invited to the great banquet.
+ Give thanks to God for your call to follow Jesus, for this call brings you into the centre of life and death.

God the merciful, we pray for all those who are marginalized and oppressed. We confess that we do not always know who these people are in our communities and even in our own congregation. Open our eyes and our hearts to the suffering of those around us, so that we follow Christ in reaching out to help and heal those in need. Give us strength to work to end the injustices that cause oppression. Make us mercy-filled. In your liberating name we pray. Amen.

DAY 74, THURSDAY

And so, with Mary Magdalene and Peter
and all the witnesses of the resurrection,
with earth and sea and all their creatures,
and with angels and archangels, cherubim and
*   seraphim,*
we praise your name and join their unending hymn.[7]

PAUSE AND REFLECT

The eucharist is a communion table. Through Christ we are connected to all people who eat this meal—our siblings in Christ, part of the household of God. We are connected to God's children around the world. God's family is our family.

The meal connects us to the whole of creation. The bread and wine are symbols of all life joining in praise of God. We humans are just a part of this song. The earth, the sea, and all their creatures join in this praise. The meal is universal, or as some Indigenous people say, it includes all our relations, every living thing.

The meal also connects us to angels, and to the saints who have gone before us.

The meal makes no distinction between people. God invites all to come and share in this mystery. All receive the same bread and wine. All are equals as they stand before the grace of God.

The meal challenges all that separates us from one another and creation:

> The eucharistic celebration . . . is a constant challenge in the search for appropriate relationships in social, economic and political life. . . . All kinds of injustice, racism, separation and lack of freedom are radically challenged when we share in the body and blood of Christ.[8]

PRAY

+ Take out your life card and think about how this meal of communion challenges your family, your work, your community, and your use of the environment.
+ Pray that the meal will open you to its sense of communion in every part of your world.

◆ Take time to go for a walk and imagine the whole of creation joining the hymn of praise.

God, you bring together all living things—earth, water, plants, animals, and people—in all kinds of diversity. You call us all to join the angels in a song of praise to you. You invite us all to feast at your heavenly banquet. As we come to your communion table, make us aware of the people you invite who are not there. Inspire us to open our welcome to all. In your banqueting name we pray. Amen.

DAY 75, FRIDAY

Jesus welcomed them and was embraced by them. So the eucharistic meal is for all, including and embracing the outcast and forgotten, the lonely and lowly, the shy and the despised. All are welcome at this table of the Lord, for Christ is the host. In its equitable distribution, the eucharist constantly critiques our world and models a just means of sharing food among all.[9]

PAUSE AND REFLECT

As Christians, we know that one of our tasks is to feed the hungry. We practice doing this every week: "Take and eat." "Take and drink." This meal blesses all tables, all fields, all soup kitchens, all shared bread. Through the eucharist we are called to be about the business of feeding.

But have we separated our eucharistic table from our common life, naming one "religious" and one "secular," with no connection between the two? Tissa Balasuriya points out the need for us to recognize the oneness of life:

An agonizing question presents itself to our minds. Why is it that in spite of the hundreds of thousands of eucharistic celebrations, Christians continue as selfish as before? Why have the "Christian" peoples been the most cruel colonizers of human history? Why is the gap of income, wealth, knowledge, and power growing in the world today—and that in favor of the "Christian" peoples? Why is it that persons and people who proclaim eucharistic love and sharing deprive the poor people of the world of food, capital, employment, and even land? Why do they prefer cigarettes and liquor to food and drink for the one-third of humanity that goes hungry to bed each night? Why are cars, cosmetics, pet dogs, horses, and bombs preferred to human children?[10]

We are called to be part of renewing the church, so that all may celebrate the oneness of the eucharist and daily life.

PRAY

+ Pray for the church, that worship and daily life can be one.
+ Pray for those who are hungry and starving.

✦ Give thanks for all who work to supply daily bread.

God of judgment, we bow before you and confess the ways in which we have left your table and then forgotten your economy, your justice, your welcome, your inclusion. We have thought only of our personal gain. We confess that we have allowed institutions, businesses, and governments to follow selfish ways too. Give us courage to repent. Forgive us and make our hearts generous and selfless. Embolden us to speak truth to power that would oppress. Help us share what we receive at your table with all your children and all creation. Trusting in your mercy, we pray. Amen.

DAY 76, SATURDAY

This cup is the new covenant in my blood,
shed for you and for all people
for the forgiveness of sin. (SC)

PAUSE AND REFLECT

At each eucharistic meal you attend, you are invited to accept that your sins are forgiven—all the callousness and neglect, all the hurt and pain that you have caused. Persistent habits of retaliation, waste, and abuse are forgiven. No sin will separate you from Christ.

There is something pernicious in us, however, that whispers, "It isn't so! Forgiveness must be earned." Or, "I know Christ forgives everyone else, but I don't believe that includes me." Remember, forgiveness is a gift for you. In Christ you are set free from your sin. Can you forgive yourself? God has; why is it hard for you?

When you stand, kneel, or sit at the table each week, remember that the people who accompany you are also forgiven. This joyous truth is due to the grace and love of God that we have come to know in Christ. In the Lord's Prayer we pray, "Forgive us our trespasses, as we forgive those who trespass against us." This is the call for us as we leave the table. Can we forgive others?

PRAY

+ Take out your life card and think of the hurt others have caused in your family, your work, your community, and the environment. Can you forgive them?

+ Stop and consider the people whom you have been unable to forgive. Try to see them through the eyes of Christ. What does Christ want to say to them? What can you say to them?

+ Pray to God for the grace to forgive. Ask God to help you in this transformation, that you may be a person who forgives.

Forgiving God, help us to glimpse your grace, mercy, and love, so that we know in our minds and hearts that you indeed forgive us and everyone around us. Teach us how to forgive others. Give us the grace to let go of past hurts and current anger.

Fill us with your grace, love, and mercy, so that they overflow to those around us. In your overflowing forgiveness we pray. Amen.

DAY 77, SUNDAY

Today is the day for the community. Prepare yourself to meet the Christ. Jesus will be present in the word and the sacraments. You will also encounter siblings in the body of Christ. Prepare to meet them. Find out how the mission of others and your mission fit together. Reflect on the meditations of the past week and what you have learned about the Lord's supper.

PRAY

God our mother hen who gathers her chicks under her wings, prepare us as you gather us together at your table today. Help us to look with your love and forgiveness on each one who comes to feast on your bounty, and to notice which of your children are not present. Move us to true hospitality and welcome, so that all may come and receive from your abundant grace. Strengthen us through your holy meal, so that we may live out your ways of justice and liberty in our lives. In your mothering name we pray. Amen.

DAY 78, MONDAY

*By Baptism we are all equally members of the
Body. Where else in this world but in the Eucharist
are king and beggar given the same gifts?*[11]

PAUSE AND REFLECT

There is a miracle happening at the eucharistic table. God sees all in the same way. All genders, all ages are the same. All states of health, all kinds of ability, all races, all occupations, all sexualities—everyone!—all receive the same gifts at the table.

Like the children of Israel as they received the gift of manna in the wilderness— each day there was only enough for each household, and a little to spare for the neighbour and the stranger.

Like the miracle of the five loaves and two fish Jesus blessed and gave to the crowd— all who were present received and were nourished.

Like God's vision of the end of the world—all will be gathered at one banquet table to eat and be nourished.

The eucharist is the place where this dream, this hope, this reality of God is kept alive on the earth.

How can you affirm this vision in your life? Does the eucharist have something to say about shelter, food, clothing, water, and how everyone might receive what they need? Does the eucharist have something to say about wages, working conditions, health care, treatment before the law, education, and all other things that are part of the stuff of life?

PRAY

+ Give thanks for the vision that is kept alive in the eucharist.
+ Ask God to show you how this vision can be carried into your daily life.
+ Take out your life card and think of the people in your life. Remember that God looks at them with love and compassion.

Bountiful God, teach us to be satisfied with enough. As we come to your holy table and all receive the same portion and gift from your precious body and blood, inspire us to think about the ways that all things of life are distributed. Help us to generously share from the bounty that we have received, according to our true ability. Give us courage to work to change unfair practices that do not equitably distribute the basic things of life. In response to your generous heart, we pray. Amen.

DAY 79, TUESDAY

A large crowd kept following [Jesus], because they saw the signs that he was doing for the sick. . . . When he looked up and saw a large crowd coming toward him, Jesus said to Philip, "Where are we to buy bread for these people to eat?" He said this to test him, for he himself knew what he was going to do. Philip answered him, "Six months' wages would not buy enough bread for each of them to get a little." One of his disciples, Andrew, Simon Peter's brother, said to him, "There is a boy here who has five barley loaves and two fish. But what are they among so many people?" Jesus said, "Make the people sit down." Now there was a great deal of grass in the place; so they sat down, about five thousand in all. Then Jesus took the loaves, and when he had given thanks, he distributed them to those who were seated; so also the fish, as much as they wanted. When they were satisfied, he told his disciples, "Gather up the fragments left over, so that nothing may be lost." So they gathered them up, and from the fragments of the five barley loaves, left by those who had eaten, they filled twelve baskets.

John 6:2, 5-13

PAUSE AND REFLECT

Jesus taught us about the extravagance of God in many parables. The amazing bounty of the mustard seed. The power of yeast to expand the dough. The strength of salt to preserve and keep life. The hospitality of a widow who loses a coin and, when she finds it, throws a party for all to celebrate. The powerful love and forgiveness of a father who welcomes his prodigal son with open arms.

Jesus showed us the open welcome and love of God in his interactions with people. Healing the sick. Raising the dead. Eating with tax collectors and other people labelled as "sinners." Talking openly with prostitutes and adulterers. Granting mercy to people of other races. Welcoming children and healing the ailing elderly. Breaking taboos of that time by allowing a menstruating woman to touch his clothing.

Jesus pointed to the beauty and value of creation. The lilies of the field. The pearl of great price. The birds of the air. Trees and their fruit. The power of the sea and the wind. Seed and grain. Wheat and weeds. Vine and branches.

Jesus told us about the heavenly banquet and how God has invited all to come and feast. And Jesus gathered his followers at a table and fed them with bread and wine, his own body and blood. Jesus now gathers us and all of humanity to come to his table, where there is always enough to sustain everyone for the journey.

One interpretation of the feeding of the five thousand is that when the small child offered his lunch and Jesus blessed it and prepared to share it, people found the items they had been hoarding for themselves and brought those out. More bread. More fish. Figs and nuts and honey. Wine. Cheese. And with all the gifts that were offered up, there was enough for all to eat and be satisfied.

PRAY

+ Pray that you, your parish, and the church may have this understanding of God's extravagance.

+ Consider the gifts you have that will nourish others. Shall they remain hidden and unused? Shall they be offered up to others? To whom?

+ Think not only of this holy table, but of all the tables you encounter, from the board room to the school room. What can you share at these tables?

Extravagant God, you continue to shower us with gifts. You bathe us in living water. You feed us at your holy table. And you promise us a welcoming table with a banquet that provides enough for all. May we follow in your ways of hospitality and share the gifts that we have been given to feed, welcome, and care for a world that is hungry for all these things. We pray in the name of Christ, who is both our host and our meal. Amen.

DAY 80, WEDNESDAY

Gather the hopes and dreams of all;
unite them with the prayers we offer now.
Grace our table with your presence,
and give us a foretaste of the things to come.[12]

Christ has died.
Christ is risen.
Christ will come again.[13]

PAUSE AND REFLECT

The table of the Lord is a feast of hope. All the groaning of the earth is brought to this table and given hope. All the pain and suffering that people face are brought to this table and given hope. All the cries of injustice heard around the world are brought to this table and given hope. All the pain of war is brought to this table and given hope. All the hope that is present in the eyes of children is affirmed. Through this meal we are children of hope and promise.

This hope is in the Christ who shall return. This hope is in the Christ who is present in your life. The community prays:

> And that we might no longer live for ourselves, but for him who died and rose for us, he sent the Holy Spirit, his own first gift for those who believe, to complete his work in the world, and to bring to fulfillment the sanctification of all.[14]

Look at your life card today. Consider the eucharist as a sign of hope. How can you carry this hope into the world around you? How will this hope affect your family life? How will this hope affect your work? How will this hope touch your community and the environment?

The offering of your life to others is not in vain. God, who has promised to restore all things, will gather up and bless this offering.

PRAY

+ Thank God for the hope we have in Christ.

+ Ask God to help you to be an agent of hope for others.

- Consider your life card and the offering you bring to others. Give thanks for these opportunities.

O God, hope for the hopeless, we give you thanks for the healing you bring to our hurting world. You show us a future without war, without hunger, without discrimination and oppression, and this fills us with hope. Help us to share that hope through words and actions that point to your intended and final vision for our world. We pray in your holy, healing, and hopeful name. Amen.

DAY 81, THURSDAY

Our Father in heaven,
    hallowed be your name,
    your kingdom come,
    your will be done, on earth as in heaven.
Give us today our daily bread.
Forgive us our sins
    as we forgive those who sin against us.
Save us from the time of trial
    and deliver us from evil.
For the kingdom, the power,
    and the glory are yours,
    now and forever. Amen.[15]

PAUSE AND REFLECT

In the liturgy of the eucharist, the Great Thanksgiving ends with all joining in the Lord's Prayer.

Krister Stendahl wrote a meaningful paraphrase of the Lord's Prayer:

O God far above and beyond our grasp, yet close to us like a parent:

Let the time come soon when you are recognized by all as God.

That is, when you establish your supreme and good and just rule over your whole creation.

Yes, let the time come soon when your gracious plan for salvation becomes a reality on earth, as it now is in heaven.

While we wait for that day, let us already now enjoy the foretaste of the messianic banquet as we share in the bread that sustains our bodies.

In order to make us worthy of that community, forgive us what we have done wrong to our brothers and sisters as we have already forgiven those who did wrong to us; for we know that we are and must be the mutually forgiven community, your community of these end times.

And see to it that we are not tested beyond our strength, for we know that Satan can destroy us—unless you rescue us out of his ferocious grip.[16]

How does this prayer help you to understand what we are about in the eucharistic feast, and what we are about in our daily living?

PRAY

+ Pray for the gentle rule of God in your life.
+ Looking at your life card, pray for people in each area of your life.

Gracious God, holy mystery and loving parent, you gather us through baptism, you feed us on your word and at your table. You give us a vision of your future and fill us with hope. Help us to absorb your tender, nurturing, and gentle teaching, and to commit to living our lives as if your promised future is already here. Make us your just, loving, peaceful, welcoming people who assist in bringing in your just, loving, peaceful, welcoming world. In your loving name we pray. Amen.

DAY 82, FRIDAY

O bread of life from heaven,
O food to pilgrims given, O manna from above:
feed with the blessed sweetness
of your divine completeness
the souls that want and need your love.

O fount of grace redeeming,
O river ever streaming from Jesus' wounded side:
come now, your love bestowing
on thirsting souls, and flowing
till all are fully satisfied.[17]

PAUSE AND REFLECT

God's holy table and God's heavenly banquet are portrayed in many ways in paintings, in hymnody and songs, in movies and plays. Pick an image used by an artist, composer, author, or poet and reflect on it. For example, consider how God's table and the heavenly banquet are portrayed in the hymn stanzas above.

PRAY

+ Spend time today recalling what has stirred in you during the time we have focused on the eucharist. Do you see the world differently through the Christ who is host at the table?

+ In what ways has the table nourished you for your mission in your family, work, community, and the environment?

+ Ask God to help you to tell others about the gifts of the eucharist.

Christ, become our eyes, that we may see the world through your vision. Christ, become our lips, so that we can proclaim your good news. Christ, become our hearts, so that we have a more expansive and generous love for others and for creation. Christ, enter our bodies through your holy meal, so that we may act as you would act in our daily lives. Gentle teacher, we pray in the name of your way, truth, and life. Amen.

CONFESSION

DAY 83, SATURDAY

What Is Confession?

Confession consists of two parts.
One is that we confess our sins.
The other is that we receive the absolution,
that is, forgiveness,
from the pastor as from God himself
and by no means doubt but firmly believe
that our sins are thereby forgiven
before God in heaven.

WHICH SINS IS A PERSON TO CONFESS?

Before God one is to acknowledge
the guilt for all sins,
even those of which we are not aware,
as we do in the Lord's Prayer.
However, before the pastor we are to confess
only those sins of which we have knowledge
and which trouble us.

WHICH SINS ARE THESE?

Here reflect on your place in life
in light of the Ten Commandments:
whether you are father, mother, son, daughter,
master, mistress, servant;
whether you have been disobedient, unfaithful, lazy,
whether you have harmed anyone by word or deed;
whether you have stolen, neglected, wasted,
or injured anything. (SC)

PAUSE AND REFLECT

During the past weeks you have been encouraged to be open with yourself before God. You have become aware of your shortcomings. At the same time you have heard that, even with your shortcomings, God loves you.

In spite of this, you may be dragging along sins from the past like a ball and chain around your foot. The actions, the neglect, and the hurt continue to hold you back.

This is not God's intention for you. At the graveside of Lazarus, Jesus said, "Unbind him, and let him go" (John 11:44). God's wish is to free all people from the burden of their sins.

PRAY

+ Look at your life card and consider whether any past actions are weighing you down.

+ Pray to be freed of guilt and to receive God's forgiveness. Consider whether it would be helpful to talk with a pastor about this.

God, you promise to forgive us, but sometimes our stubborn hearts are not able to trust or accept this gift of grace. We confess that sometimes we don't believe that your grace extends to us. We confess that we have fallen into the trap of holding onto guilt and not forgiving ourselves. Help us to know your love and accept your forgiving embrace. Give us the joy and freedom of confessing and finally hearing and trusting your word of forgiveness. We pray with repentant and hopeful hearts. Amen.

DAY 84, SUNDAY

As you join the parish in worship on this Sunday, consider how the forgiveness of sin is proclaimed. Listen for the words of grace and assurance that come through worship.

PRAY

God, we come to worship hungry to hear your word of forgiveness. Help us to be still inside and to truly listen to your word speaking to us in liturgy, hymns, scripture, sermon, and your holy meal. As we share the peace with others, let that be a moment that affirms that we are forgiven. Enable us to share your forgiving word with those who have hurt us. We pray these things seeking your grace. Amen.

DAY 85, MONDAY

*Individual Confession and Forgiveness is a ministry
of the church through which a person may confess
sin and receive the assurance of God's forgiveness.*[1]

PAUSE AND REFLECT

God does not want to condemn, but to liberate all from the burden of sins from the past and present. If you are weighed down by your sins and find it difficult to let go of guilt and receive God's forgiveness, private confession with a pastor or friend can be helpful. Pastors are bound by the oath of ordination to maintain confidentiality. The order of Individual Confession and Forgiveness that follows may be used.

The pastor begins:
Blessed be the Holy Trinity, one God,
who forgives all our sin,
whose mercy endures forever.
Response: Amen.

You have come to make confession before God.
You are free to confess before me, a pastor in the church of Christ,
sins of which you are aware and which trouble you.

The penitent may use the following form or pray in her/his own words.
Merciful God, I confess
that I have sinned in thought, word, and deed,
by what I have done and by what I have left undone.
Here the penitent may confess sins that are known and that burden her/him.

I repent of all my sins, known and unknown.
I am truly sorry, and I pray for forgiveness.
I firmly intend to amend my life,
and to seek help in mending what is broken.
I ask for strength to turn from sin
and to serve you in newness of life.

The pastor may engage the penitent in conversation, sharing admonition, counsel, and comfort from the scriptures. Psalm 51 or 103 may be spoken together.

Addressing the penitent, the pastor may lay both hands on the penitent's head.
Cling to this promise: the word of forgiveness I speak to you comes from God.

[Name], by water and the Holy Spirit
God gives you a new birth,
and through the death and resurrection
of Jesus Christ,
God forgives you all your sins.
Almighty God
strengthen you in all goodness
and keep you in eternal life.
Response: Amen.[2]

PRAY

+ Consider the sufferings, disappointments, illnesses, struggles, and failures you have experienced. Have you borne any of these rather well, all things considered? Congratulations! Which were most painful or cost you most? Who or what supported you in these difficult times?

+ Consider the faults, sins, bad examples, hurtful words, meanness, and wrongdoings you are responsible for in different periods of your life. It may not be easy to admit them. Which do you most regret?

+ Consider that, in spite of your faults and wrongdoings, neither God nor persons have given up on you. God never will. You have everlasting, indestructible value in God's eyes. You are worth so very much.

+ Thank God and pray for the people who have stuck with you. Give thanks for the forgiveness God has shown you through it all.[3]

Loving God, give us the courage and willingness to honestly admit to our faults, sins, bad examples, hurtful words, meanness, and wrongdoings. We confess these things to you. When we hang onto these burdens, unable to feel and claim your forgiveness, be with us as we seek help through confession to a pastor or another believer. May we hear your gracious words of absolution. We thank you for those who have journeyed with us despite our faults. In your forgiving name we pray. Amen.

DAY 86, TUESDAY

Confessing our sin involves a continuing return to our baptism where our sinful self is drowned and dies; in the gift of forgiveness God raises us up again and again to new life in Jesus Christ.[4]

PAUSE AND REFLECT

Scripture encourages us to seek and offer forgiveness again and again: "When you are offering your gift at the altar, if you remember that your brother or sister has something against you, leave your gift there before the altar and go; first be reconciled to your brother or sister, and then come and offer your gift" (Matthew 5:23-24). Some have learned this from others or know it instinctively. By God's grace we seek out our siblings in Christ and ask for forgiveness or speak plainly about hurts. Knowing that God's grace constantly surrounds us, we have the freedom to take such risks on a daily basis.

PRAY

+ Give thanks for God's forgiveness and grace.

+ Pray for those with burdened consciences.

+ Look at your life card and consider what would happen if you spoke openly with others, in both confessing your sins and describing your hurts.

+ Consider the people in your life and ask God to help you make a covenant of reconciliation with them.

Reconciling God, too often we hurt or harm others, or they hurt or harm us, and we lack the will to seek reconciliation. Instead, we build up walls, enter into long and painful silences, cut off relationships, or triangulate others into our conflicts. Give us the strength and courage to seek reconciliation with those we have wronged and those who have wronged us. Give us sincere words and actions, and hearts full of humility. Help us to gracefully receive either forgiveness or rejection, but do not let us further harden our hearts. Strengthen us to strive for your peace with one another. In your overflowing forgiveness we pray. Amen.

DAY 87, WEDNESDAY

[Name],
in obedience to the command
of our Lord Jesus Christ,
I forgive you all your sins
in the name of the Father,
and of the Son,
and of the Holy Spirit.[5]

PAUSE AND REFLECT

No sin, however gross or grievous to you and others, stands outside the light of God's forgiveness. You are forgiven in the name of the Father, and of the Son, and of the Holy Spirit. Those same words used in baptism are now yours again. All is forgiven.

This forgiveness from God invites you to seek reconciliation with others. They may be unwilling to forgive; remember how you have been unwilling to forgive others. They may not be ready to forgive; you must be patient with them as God has been patient with you. Continue to hope and pray for reconciliation.

Consider Jesus' words from the cross: "Father, forgive them; for they do not know what they are doing" (Luke 23:34). Will you forgive others as a servant of Christ, or will you carry those hurts the rest of your life and force others to bear their sins for the rest of their lives?

PRAY

+ Speak to another about your hurt and your feelings of resentment.

+ Ask God to show you the way to healing and the forgiveness of others.

+ Take out your life card and consider the people in your life. If there are people whom you find it impossible to forgive, is God calling you to see things differently?

+ Remember all of the people who have stuck with you throughout your life and forgiven you. Give thanks for these people.

+ Ask God to give you a spirit of compassion and forgiveness.

Christ who forgave from the cross, you show us the way to live towards forgiveness and reconciliation. We give you thanks for all the people you have placed in our lives who have forgiven us our sins and wrongdoings. Encourage us with their example of love that bears all things. Kindle within us the fire of both giving and receiving forgiveness. In your reconciling name we pray. Amen.

CONCLUSION

DAY 88, THURSDAY

[Jesus said,] "For it is as if a man, going on a journey, summoned his slaves and entrusted his property to them; to one he gave five talents, to another two, to another one, to each according to his ability. Then he went away. The one who had received the five talents went off at once and traded with them, and made five more talents. In the same way, the one who had the two talents made two more talents. But the one who had received the one talent went off and dug a hole in the ground and hid his master's money. After a long time the master of those slaves came and settled accounts with them. Then the one who had received the five talents came forward, bringing five more talents, saying, 'Master, you handed over to me five talents; see, I have made five more talents.' His master said to him, 'Well done, good and trustworthy slave; you have been trustworthy in a few things, I will put you in charge of many things; enter into the joy of your master.' . . . Then the one who had received the one talent also came forward, saying, 'Master, I knew that you were a harsh man, reaping where you did not sow, and gathering where you did not scatter seed; so I was afraid, and I went and hid your talent in the ground. Here you have what is yours.' But his master replied, 'You wicked and lazy slave! You knew, did you, that I reap where I did not sow, and gather where I did not scatter? Then you ought to have invested my money with the bankers, and on my return I would have received what was my own with interest. So take the talent from him, and give it to the one with the ten talents.'"

Matthew 25:14-21, 24-28

PAUSE AND REFLECT

As you conclude these days of prayer, look again at the matter of the gifts and talents that God has given you and how you are to use them.

In this parable the man gives the servants complete freedom to do what they wish with the gifts given to them, inviting them to be people of risk and to use their abilities for the sake of the master's work. They can exercise their gifts in freedom and joy. This is God's intention for you.

When we read or hear this parable, many of us focus on the third servant: "I knew you were a harsh man . . . and I went and hid your talent in the ground." You may deeply sympathize with this person. You too may know the fear of failure and therefore do not make use of the talents and gifts that God has given you. But consider the God whom you serve. Is this God like the many people in our society who demand conformity? Or is this God one who loves you and gives you freedom to act out of your true heart's desire?

PRAY

+ Spend time in your prayers celebrating the love and freedom to act that God has given you.
+ Ask God to take away any fears that prevent you from acting in freedom.
+ Pray for others in your parish to be able to act freely out of God's great love for them.

Generous God, you gift us all differently with talents and gifts. Help us to honour what you have given us by not comparing our gifts with those of others. Who we are and what we have are gifts from you, so we know they are good and they are enough. Free us from the fear of failure, and enable us to use and develop our gifts and talents. Send your discerning Spirit to show us how best to use our gifts as part of your plan to love and save the world. We pray with hearts full of thankfulness. Amen.

DAY 89, FRIDAY

Rejoice in the Lord always; again I will say, Rejoice. Let your gentleness be known to everyone. The Lord is near. Do not worry about anything, but in everything by prayer and supplication with thanksgiving let your requests be made known to God. And the peace of God, which surpasses all understanding, will guard your hearts and your minds in Christ Jesus.

Philippians 4:4-7

PAUSE AND REFLECT

During the last several weeks you have taken time for daily meditation and prayer. Will you be able to continue this discipline?

In our busy lives, it is hard to maintain daily prayer and meditation. It is much easier to postpone this time, thinking that maybe we will start again "next week" when we are not as busy. Look for ways to encourage yourself and to be encouraged by others in this daily discipline.

Scripture contains much encouragement to pray. Jesus was well versed in the Hebrew Scriptures and spent a great deal of quiet time with God, even in the moments before his trial and death. Martin Luther, who called the church and believers to deeper spirituality, spent three hours each day reading the scriptures, meditating, and praying. He often said that if he did not take time for this, he would never get his work done!

PRAY

+ Reflect on the past weeks and the ways in which meditation and prayer have added to your life. Think of people in your parish or in your family who would be able to encourage you in this discipline.
+ Give thanks for God's presence in your life and the times you have been made aware of that presence.
+ Give thanks for the writings and example of Martin Luther.

God, you breathe into us at our creation, you breathe your Spirit into us at baptism, and you continue to breathe love and grace and forgiveness into our lives. How can we do anything else but love and adore you? Strengthen us to spend time each day in devotion towards and meditation on your never-ending love. In our times of prayer and meditation, help us to breathe deeply of your promises and exhale all that would tear us away from you. We pray, resting in your love. Amen.

DAY 90, SATURDAY

*Now the eleven disciples went to Galilee, to the
mountain to which Jesus had directed them. When
they saw him, they worshiped him; but some doubted.
And Jesus came and said to them, "All authority
in heaven and on earth has been given to me. Go
therefore and make disciples of all nations, baptizing
them in the name of the Father and of the Son and of
the Holy Spirit, and teaching them to obey everything
that I have commanded you. And remember, I am
with you always, to the end of the age."*

Matthew 28:16-20

PAUSE AND REFLECT

There is much wisdom in reflection. Martin Buber, a Jewish theologian, encouraged
anyone who had learned something new to first carry it around for a while. Let the
new thing push against the inner boundaries of the soul—like someone pregnant
with new life. Then, when you do begin telling others about it, it's like giving birth
to the new child in you.

During the past ninety days you have placed yourself before God each day. God has
been at work within you, calling you to a new life in Christ. Something new may be
taking shape in your life in terms of how you might serve this God.

If you have discovered a new way in which you feel called to follow Jesus, perhaps it
is time to tell the community of faith. To make this announcement is to invite the
community's prayers and help in fulfilling this calling.

Love and serve God and all of God's creation, knowing that as the early disciples
were sent out with Jesus' blessing, so are you.

PRAY

+ Take out your life card and pray that every area of your life may be lived under
  the promise of God.

God of the beginning of time, God of the end of all ages, you promise to be with us always. Help us to rest securely in that promise, knowing that you are always near, always loving, always forgiving. Show us how to live each day, knowing that in all our thoughts and actions you are before us, behind us, above us, below us, and within us. We love you, we love you, we love you. With hearts full of your grace, we pray. Amen.

NOTES

SECTION I

No Other Gods . . . The Ten Commandments

1. *Evangelical Lutheran Worship [ELW]* (Minneapolis: Augsburg Fortress, 2006), 235.

2. *ELW*, 252.

I Believe . . . The Apostles' Creed

1. *ELW*, 107.

2. Chief Qwatsinas, "Chief Qwatsinas on Forests (17 October 2009)," http://www.nuxalk.net/html/forests.htm.

3. *ELW*, 69.

4. Johann Heermann; tr. Robert Bridges, alt., "Ah, holy Jesus," ELW 349, sts. 4 and 5.

5. *ELW*, 231.

6. Text of verses 1 and 6 of "I Was There to Hear Your Borning Cry" © 1985 John C. Ylvisaker. Used by permission of Fern M. Kruger.

Teach Us to Pray . . . The Lord's Prayer

1. "Walls that divide," *Songs for a Gospel People* (Winfield, BC: Wood Lake Books, 1987), 32–33, refrain. Text and music © 1974 Walter Farquharson.

SECTION II

Baptism

1. *ELW*, 231.

2. Barbara M. Joosse, *Mama, Do You Love Me?* (San Francisco: Chronicle Books, 1991).

3. *ELW*, 229.

4. *ELW*, 230.

5. *ELW*, 98.

6. *ELW*, 231.

7. "This is the Spirit's entry now," ELW 448. Text © Thomas E. Herbranson, admin. Augsburg Fortress.

8. *ELW*, 231.

9. Gordon W. Lathrop, *Living Witnesses: The Adult Catechumenate, Congregational Prayers to Accompany the Catechumenal Process* (Winnipeg: Evangelical Lutheran Church in Canada, 1992), 9–10.

10. *ELW*, 231.

11. *ELW*, 231.

12. *ELW*, 87.

Holy Communion

1. *ELW*, 106.

2. *ELW*, 107.

3. *The Book of Alternative Services of the Anglican Church of Canada* (Toronto: Anglican Book Centre, 1985), 128.

4. Martin Luther, tr. Jeremiah J. Schindel, rev. E. Theodore Bachman, "The Blessed Sacrament of the Holy and True Body of Christ and the Brotherhoods, 1519," *Luther's Works* (Philadelphia: Muhlenberg Press, 1960), 35:59–60.

5. *Luther's Works*, 35:54.

6. Jürgen Moltmann, *The Church in the Power of the Spirit* (New York: Harper & Row, 1977), 258.

7. *Evangelical Lutheran Worship Leaders Desk Edition* (Minneapolis: Augsburg Fortress, 2006), 187.

8. World Council of Churches Commission on Faith and Order, *Baptism, Eucharist and Ministry* (Geneva: World Council of Churches, 1982), 101.

9. J. Frank Henderson, Kathleen Quinn, Stephen Larson, *Liturgy, Justice and the Reign of God: Integrating Vision and Practice* (Mahwah, NJ: Paulist, 1989), 102.

10. Tissa Balasuriya, *The Eucharist and Human Liberation* (Maryknoll, NY: Orbis Books, 1979), xi–xii.

11. Louis Weil, in *Liturgy, Justice and the Reign of God*, 104.

12. "Let the vineyards be fruitful," ELW 182. Text © 1978 *Lutheran Book of Worship*, admin. Augsburg Fortress.

13. *ELW*, 109.

14. *The Book of Alternative Services*, 208.

15. *ELW,* 112.

16. Krister Stendahl, "The Lord's Prayer—A Paraphrase," in *The Kingdom on Its Way: Meditations for Music and Mission* (Geneva: World Council of Churches, 1980), 81–82.

17. Latin hymn, c. 1661; tr. Hugh T. Henry, 1862–1946, sts. 1, 3; tr. Philip Schaff, 1819–1893, st. 2, "O bread of life from heaven," ELW 480, sts. 1 and 2.

Confession

1. *ELW,* 243.

2. *ELW,* 243–244.

3. These questions are based upon Richard J. Huelsman, *Pray: Step-by-Step Directions and Guidance for Praying* (Mahwah, NJ: Paulist Press, 1976), 9–10.

4. *ELW,* 243.

5. *ELW,* 244.